Gay & Healthy
in a Sick Society

The Minor Details

Robert N. Minor, Ph.D.

HumanityWorks!
A CONSORTIUM BUILDING:

Published by HumanityWorks!
4047 Botanical Avenue, Suite 200
St. Louis, MO 63110-3905
1-314-771-1908, Humanitywks@aol.com

Publisher's Cataloging-in-Publication
(Provided by Quality Books, Inc.)

Minor, Robert Neil, 1945-
  Gay & healthy in a sick society : the minor details /
by Robert N. Minor.
    p. cm.
    LCCN: 2003096255
    ISBN: 0-9709581-1-0

    1. Homosexuality--United States. 2. Gays--United
States--Social conditions. 3. Homophobia--United
States. 4. Sex role --United States.   I. Title.

HQ76.3.U5M539 2003   306.76'6
                        QBI03-200716

"Anger" by Mahrya Monson used with permission.
Photography, cover design, and book layout by Gary Rockhold.

For more information visit: www.fairnessproject.org

Contents

Introduction

The student sitting across from me in my campus office was using a lot of effort to explain why he was barely passing my "Living Religions of the East" course. Anyone could have concluded as much from his constantly shifting posture and intense facial expressions.

But as he explained his case, I didn't believe him. My instincts or experience as a teacher, or something else I'm not sure of, convinced me that he was actually very bright. I've taught long enough to know when I'm being snowed.

Still, as he spoke, he described himself with a pattern of self-defeating words throughout his appeals. Basically, he said, he was a hard worker, but just not very smart.

Falling back on my professorial role as a historian, I asked him for proof. Did he have any objective data to support the conclusion that he was as naturally unintelligent as he said he was?

"Just my past university grades. My mom read to me when I was young and I really liked to read as a kid. My family thought I was 'the smart one.' My sisters teased me about it. And I started out really well in grade school."

I decided to push a bit. "So, what's your earliest memory of someone important who told you that you weren't very smart?"

It actually took little time for him to remember a third grade teacher. The man seemed larger than life to the young boy. And to the third grader, the teacher seemed to add consistently an explanation to their conversations: "You're just one of those people who aren't very smart."

I learned that the student's authoritative evaluator was a teacher in the small, rural community where he grew up. As an elementary and secondary student, he was from one of the few Hispanic families in a very white town. And he was the only Hispanic boy in his elementary school.

I asked if he had ever considered that what the teacher told him was actually the result of the teacher's learned prejudices. Did the teacher just assume that Hispanic boys were intellectually inferior? And was that an absolutely false message the young boy had internalized, a message that had nothing to do with him and everything to do with systemic racial prejudices?

For some reason, that was a new thought for him. He had never considered it. A new way of understanding what had happened struck him, and his eyes deepened. All of a sudden, he was faced with considering the possibility that he was not the real problem. The problem was a system that didn't accept deviants from its ideal: an image of whiteness.

In that case, then, he was actually okay. In reality, the system, represented by that authority figure and "role model," had a huge problem. The system and its teaching were sick and wrong. But it was telling an eight year old boy that he was the problem.

That's a dominant message propagated by any cultural system. Every institution that's successful in a society supports the foundational messages that the system teaches its children from the moment they are born. And children hear few alternatives to these foundational messages.

A thriving system never teaches that there's something deeply wrong with it, even if it's fatally ill. Okay, it says, it's probably not perfect. We may need to tinker with the system a bit. But we shouldn't question the system itself. The problem is always identified as anyone who deviates from its ideals. As our media often frame it, one of our problems, for example, is not white racism, but our culture's "minority problem."

Individuals who question things and don't exhibit and value the characteristics that the system says are best, are supposed to believe they are crazy, valueless, even dangerous nonconformists. But society? It's just fine, thank you.

So while society grinds on in its usual fashion, people are taught to fit in and to consider themselves the problem when they don't fit. Blaming individuals who aren't white enough, pretty enough, masculine enough, able-bodied enough, rich enough, or straight enough, keeps the system from turning attention onto itself and the problems created by its core teachings. The system and its beneficiaries prefer not to evaluate themselves.

To keep the system going, those of us living in it internalize and act the standard roles we are expected to play as man and woman. Playing them has its rewards. Deviating from them is punished.

No matter what our ethnic or racial background, if we want to succeed we are supposed to be white-acting, white-thinking, white-feeling, and as white-looking as possible. If we are, then we'll succeed somewhat in the institutions about us that reward us monetarily and with a sense of community and acceptance.

No matter what our sexual orientation — heterosexual, bisexual, homosexual, or uncertain-sexual — we are expected to live a role that is "straight." All of us are supposed to be straight-acting, straight-thinking, straight-feeling, and straight-looking. And the consequences of not fitting in to "straightness" can be violence, threats of violence, ridicule, humiliation, isolation, and rejection. I have discussed what this means and how our fear-based system's values are installed in us in a previous book: *Scared Straight: Why It's So Hard to Accept Gay People and Why It's So Hard to Be Human.* (St. Louis: Humanity Works!, 2001)

This straight role is dominant because it works. It works to keep things going. It works to keep a system in place in our country, a system that is profit-oriented, not human-oriented, a system that is oriented to coping, not healing.

Who hasn't noticed how important profits are in our society? We've developed a culture and standard of living so tied to such a high level of money-making that many of our core values, even our lives, are dependent upon monetary success. We've been told that what's good for big business (often called "the economy") is good for all of us. Anyone who argues differently is suspect.

We don't believe that guaranteeing the health of every human being who is a U.S. citizen is an asset worth whatever it takes. We're afraid it might cost too much and threaten the profits of the insurance industry.

Clean air and water that won't kill us must not cost our industries too much. We talk of considering a "cost-benefit ratio." We hope that someday, and who knows how many cancer deaths later, technology will find a way to do it that won't cost too much.

And peace? Well, we have to take into consideration that peace might close our defense industries and put people out of work. We're financially committed to a war economy because peace might cost too much. But it doesn't matter how much war costs — war is always worth it.

To maintain the status quo, our system is also oriented to coping, not healing. We must figure out and support ways to get by, put up with, get along, and sedate ourselves so we can make it till death catches us.

From many of our mainstream psychological professionals to most of our society-approved addictions, the goal is far from identifying the system as crazy-making and changing it. System-approved and authorized approaches target possible deviants as threats to the system. Then their goal is to help them fit in. They identify the problem as the individual who doesn't keep the system going. They label these outsiders useless and crazy. They marginalize and warehouse them. And the media paint them out with system-affirming brush strokes.

Psychologist and author Ann Wilson Schaef was one of these system-affirming psychotherapists. She came to realize that psychotherapy was really meant to identify the problem as the individual's inability to fit in. Its goal was to change the individual's wishes, hopes, expectations, and dreams so that they can make it in the structures. In particular, Schaef was working with women who could not fit happily into a system that was male-dominated and that valued ways to do things that were "masculine." Her goal was to get them to cope, to go along. Health was defined as doing what affirmed and maintained the system.

Schaef's book, *Women's Reality* (3rd ed, 1992) arose out of her realization that the values of the system itself are the real problem. They are inhuman. At first she thought that it was just that women saw things differently from men, but soon she came to understand that the system itself was very sick. In fact, the system was the disease, a disease she identified as an addiction. Her book *When Society Becomes An Addict* (1988) was the result of this change of perspective.

Coping with the system was unhealthy, she concluded. People who coped were like an addict's enabler, enabling the addict to continue in the addictive behavior until the addict and all around are destroyed by the addiction.

With this realization, Schaef became one of the growing number of those who call themselves recovering psychotherapists. No longer is her goal to help human beings cope but to promote real individual and societal healing.

There are a lot of the more obvious coping mechanisms. They are also, not coincidentally, profit-making. And when they get out of hand, by the system's definition, there are even profits in controlling them.

In these extreme forms there are even system-affirming groups and institutions to support our coping with the addiction and the system. They help individuals remove the excesses of one addiction or another without questioning the system, or the need to cope itself.

Even if someone doesn't qualify as an alcoholic, the need for a drink after work helps one cope with the job. Without that drink (or two, or three) to sedate the feelings of frustration, alienation, meaninglessness, helplessness, and sense of being demeaned that one experiences in what occupies most of our waking hours, the raw misery might eventually lead to the desire to change things and the system they support.

Work itself is a system-approved addiction because it keeps workers working, or over-working. We talk about, and even laugh about, workaholics, but we continue on as if it's healthy. Who would have thought that "overtime" would ever be considered a benefit for workers, as it often is today?

Work and other distractions help us cope with problems in our personal lives, problems with our families, or negative feelings about our personal accomplishments. So, often we feel better at work than in what could be our most intimate relationships. Such addictions may not catch up with us but, as the old saying goes: "No one on their deathbed ever said, 'I wish I'd have spent more time at the office.'"

The system also teaches us to believe that what is good for this system is good for human beings. We not only embrace that idea but come to defend it, even when we are the ones being laid off in its name.

This all recalls the classic arguments of Adam Smith for capitalism. Unable to explain how it will really do what's right for the majority of people, he speaks of an "invisible hand" of capitalism that's supposed to take care of what a profit-oriented system can't logically produce for most human beings. In other words, he has no real explanation. We're to just have faith.

In fact, we're really supposed to be afraid that there is no good, positive, healthier alternative to our system. In response to criticisms of the way things are, people often ask "Well, what's the alternative?" Yet they're not asking that question with a serious, open intention of hearing alternatives but with a hopeless feeling that there aren't any.

That's what the citizens of the ancient Roman Empire believed too. If you lived in those days of what was called "Pax Romana," you were convinced that, maybe with some minor tinkering, the Roman system was the best that things could ever be. There seemed to be no viable alternatives. So the fall of Rome would be the end of any hope. Like any system, the Roman socio-economic-educational-political-religious system had convinced its citizens that the only alternative to it was chaos, destruction, disease, and death.

The fear of "barbarian" invasions, the take-over by people who must be uncivilized since their civilization was not like the Roman one, came to loom on the horizon. It scared Romans further into enacting stricter laws and punishments, promoting more conservative measures, espousing restrictive moralisms, fearing and blaming outsiders, increasing surveillance, and raising a religious (which near the end became a "Christian") backlash.

But it eventually happened. Rome fell. Those "barbarians" invaded. "Civilization" as they knew it came to an end. And the world went on to other alternatives which Rome's leaders had never conceived. They couldn't have, for a successfully installed system takes away from grown-ups what its children had — the comfort and love of dreaming really creative, radical, and system-challenging dreams of what could be. Such dreams, children are soon taught, are impractical, unreal, inefficient, and won't help you get ahead (in the system as it is).

The deviants are the people outside the straight role that we're all supposed to live. They may be of any sexual orientation, uncertain, heterosexual, bisexual, or homosexual. But when they live outside the accepted role they are all in some sense "queer."

Gay people have decided that based solely upon whom they love, they are in some sense outside the role. Once they've made this decision, they can do everything possible to mimic the straight role, to act as if they really aren't different from straight people. They can do all they can to participate in the cultural sickness. And, given that they are conditioned to live in the victim role, they are also supposed to believe that down deep in some way they will never be able to fully live as straight.

Or gay people can see themselves as healthy *because* they are outside the dominant role. They can decide to redefine the values of the culture so as to be agents of healing. They can recognize that a culture that minimizes them is really laden with straight problems.

It's the possible choice of anyone not to conform to "straight." Many heterosexual people are deciding not to conform. They're choosing new ways of relating, new forms of partnering and commitment, and even new ways to experience commitment ceremonies. While some gay people are seeking to fit in, to cope, to ape, to lose their chance to heal, other people of all sexual orientations have recognized the sickness around them that's ultimately destructive of all creatures and the planet itself.

Our culture needs the perspective that people outside the role have to offer. And it will be a different perspective than that installed by our straight-acting cultural institutions.

A drag queen walked into a high Roman Catholic mass one Sunday morning and sat down. She watched with fascination as the priest walked down the aisle in full robes, swinging a smoking censor of incense.

As he passed her pew, she couldn't help herself. "Nice dress honey," she said to the priest, "but your purse is on fire."

There were two perspectives at the edge of that pew in that mass at that moment. The priest's was the official and learned view. The drag queen saw the whole scene quite differently. The first took the scene as it had been understood for generations, convinced that it was *the* right way to do so. The second perspective saw everything from outside of the conventional ways of seeing it. The first knew how to "correctly" and "appropriately" explain the scene. The second raised a whole new set of questions about the reality around it.

There are many ways of seeing the society we live in, some conventional, and some fresh and even critical. The conventional maintains the status quo. In its numbing repetition it drowns out other, often healthier, ways of seeing the same things. But the fresh opens us to new possibilities.

That's what the following essays are about. They were first written as a column entitled "Minor Details" for the Kansas monthly LGBT magazine, *Liberty Press*. More recently they have also been made available on the web as viewpoints in the acclaimed daily national newsmagazine *Gay Today*.

They were written as monthly columns, not as a standard book. So, as columns they could not assume that someone had read the previous columns, nor could they assume people had not. Some repetition was necessary to ensure that new readers each month were with them. When they are collected, especially by topic, as they are in this collection, the repetition is more obvious, but, I think, still helpful.

At the request of many regular readers as well as some who had only read one or two columns, I have pulled most of them together in this collection. I have made only a few changes and tried to organize them thematically.

Little of what I write is new. It's just what I've learned. I have learned much from readers. I have sometimes been scolded and praised, most often thanked. Since I am always learning, all the comments have helped.

I have also made friends with some wonderful people as a result. *Liberty Press* editors Kristi Parker and Vinnie Levine, and *Gay Today* editor, author, and veteran activist Jack Nichols, to name a few, have encouraged and greatly supported me. When I was initially writing them I often read them to a good friend, Rev. Paul Smith, who didn't hesitate to give me what was very good feedback. I owe much to Brenda Bobo-Fisher and Mahrya Monson of HumanityWorks! Their faith in me is a reflection of both their commitments to real love and justice. I also thank Toby Johnson for his recent support. And no one has been more supportive day after day than Gary Rockhold. Thank you all.

I put these ideas forth again in response to readers' requests, and with the solid conviction that we live in a society that is sick and needs much healing. I also remain convinced that lesbians, gay men, and bisexual and transgender people are just fine. I believe that they have much to offer to heal our critically ill system. I also believe that they are healthy to the extent that they do not conform to, but reject, the sickness that tries to convince us to go-along, conform, assimilate, partake of, and live off of all the sick institutions around us.

The call of LGBT prophets who see things differently can lead us to new institutions. But it can do so only if these potential new role models don't give up all that they have to offer the world in order to get along. This book is dedicated to all who don't give up.

Our Self-Image

The Minor Details

What's the Value of
LGBT Consumers?

Touting the LGBT community, particularly its white males, as a group that spends a larger disposable income has been a strategy for marketing and advertising for decades. Mainstream businesses and advertisers, though often slow to get the profit-making implications of the message, have responded by targeting the dollars of gay and lesbian consumers.

Opinions about the actual nature of the market range from denial that LGBT people are actually economically better off, to surveys that are often skewed to questioning only those from upper-income brackets. The research seems to support all the claims.

Reliable surveys have also shown a sizeable gap between the earnings and disposable income spending habits of gay male and lesbian couples. The difference reflects the overall gap in income between men and women in our society, doubled by the fact that two male incomes are being compared with two female incomes. There's no surprise here, since in the U.S. women still make no more than 75 cents for every dollar made by men in the same position.

For those who celebrate such things, it's clear that our worth is in our pocketbooks. Being courted by marketers has little if anything to with the value of LGBT individuals and their relationships. It has everything to do with the bottom line. It's how much money we keep earning and how willing we are to continue consuming.

This is no more blatantly clear than in documents recently uncovered by the American Legacy Foundation, a public health foundation that emerged from the 1998 tobacco companies' legal settlement with a number of states. In the documents, food and tobacco giant R.J. Reynolds speaks of targeting San Francisco's LGBT consumers in the 1990's with "Project SCUM," short for "Subculture Urban Marketing." In the master plan, America's largest tobacco manufacturer strategizes its marketing to the LGBT community whose rates of smoking are far above the national average. LGBT people are "scum" valuable only as a market.

Right-wing religious and political extremists agree with the more optimistic economic assertions of the marketers. They leap upon claims of our greater income and spending potential as evidence to argue that LGBT people aren't real victims of discrimination. No changes are needed, they say, because we are, in fact, rich beneficiaries of society just the way it is. We're actually a privileged group living off the fat of the land. So, why would LGBT people need any legal protections?

Other groups that have experienced discrimination have often characterized us similarly. So, when we compare anti-gay oppression with white racism, people of color picture gay people as rich, white whiners who wouldn't know real oppression if it hit them in their overly fat pocketbooks.

The latest salvo in the campaign to court us economically has been fired with Richard Florida's new book: *The Rise of the Creative Class: And How it's Transforming Work, Leisure, Community and Everyday Life* (Basic Books, 2002). Florida is on the current high-end business luncheon circuit advising cities that their future is tied to their ability to attract people who "create meaningful new forms."

This "creative class" includes not only scientists, engineers, architects, and university professors, but artists, poets, novelists, entertainers, actors, designers, and other cultural figures. Cities that attract them no longer follow the usual strategies to recruit more companies in the hope of becoming the next Silicone Valley, or building professional sports stadiums, or developing retail complexes. They have begun to recognize demographic changes that make young people, singles, new immigrants, and gay people critical contributors to the social fabric. They are known to be open to diversity and are actively and publicly working to cultivate it.

Now, to most of us it takes little imagination to conclude that such cities must come to value, not merely tolerate, LGBT people along with non-straight-acting heterosexuals who feel safer in places that welcome queer people. Florida says so in his writings. His "Creativity Index" measures diversity by: "the Gay Index, a reasonable proxy for an area's openness to different kinds of people and ideas." In fact, an article based on his book is subtitled "Why cities without gays and rock bands are losing the economic development race."

This is not only good news for LGBT people. It's good news for everyone who finds little attraction in white-bread suburbs, slick malls, big box retail stores, cookie-cutter houses, and fake replicas of buildings with character.

If our cities would take Florida's advice, inner cities would continue to revive historic buildings, established neighborhoods, and older downtown retail, manufacturing, and living complexes. What this creative class is attracted to, he argues, is an authentic sense of the inner cities, and what developers in the past have considered grit.

Of course, in reality many LGBT people are attracted to the suburban gentry lifestyle. They find comfort in tidy, straight coupling places that claim to be "good locations for raising a family." They are targetable consumers of affluence. And they want to blend into "the good life" represented by suburbia. They might even become the "Joneses" everyone should keep up with.

Unless they're willing to move into established inner-city neighborhoods that include large and stately homes, Florida's recommendations won't mean much to them personally. They may even join those who complain about the city, though they may be attracted to the diversity of clubs and the colorful culture only urban cores provide.

The message? People who might otherwise see no value in us should grit their teeth and tolerate LGBT people because they have financial worth. It's an appealing argument in a profit-oriented culture with an addictive need to maintain a fast-paced economy.

And no matter how successful Florida's admonitions to community and business leaders are when he says that LGBT people do have a value, it has to strike us that such appeals are not about the value of people we love. They are not about our value as human beings or our inherent right to all the benefits straight people have. They are not really about our cultural contributions. And they are not about what we can offer a very sick society as alternatives to its failed values and institutions.

Florida's arguments will also work as long as no one realizes that the majority of LGBT people are working-class people who struggle along with other working-class people.

Yet this approach is only dangerous to us when we believe that what we are worth is tied to our consumerist capabilities. It's then that we value ourselves and each other on the basis of what we drive, how large our houses are, and whether we fit into a lifestyle defined by how much we spend. When we do that, we prove we're just as sick and lost as the greater society struggling around us.

Teletubbies 'R Us

It's no surprise that the counsel from right-wing Rev. Jerry Falwell's magazine is homophobic, heterosexist, and oppressive of gay, lesbian, bisexual and transgender human beings. But we are less likely to notice that many "enlightened" responses to Falwell may also be homophobic, heterosexist, and oppressive.

The non-homophobic, non-heterosexist response to the idea that TV's Teletubby Tinky Winky is gay would have been "And your point is?" or "And so?" But hidden in attempts to deny it is the implicit belief that being gay would be a bad thing. Instead, the response seems to be that if he were he should be in the closet; but, be assured children, he's not.

Phew! We don't have to worry. Our children are safe after all.

The responses were also often thoroughly gender conditioned. Since the Teletubbies have no obvious genitalia, it's curious to speak of a voice "like a man" and "carrying a purse." The denial that Tinky Winky has a "purse," — it's a "magic bag" — whether it is or not, was swift. We certainly don't want children to think that low-voiced beings (who must surely, then, be male) carry purses (which surely is a female thing).

That this is more silly, American homophobia and gender conditioning is the issue. Remember the Seinfeld episode where people accused Jerry of "carrying a purse," and he constantly reminded them: "It's not a purse, it's European." Surely, unlike Europe, we are one of the most homophobic, most tightly gender conditioned, civilizations on the planet, and think that's just how it should be.

Such responses are even internalized in the LGBT community. Every time one of us responds to those who deny us equality, with the argument that our acceptance should be based on the fact that we wouldn't choose being LGBT if we could, we are speaking out of our internalized oppression.

No doubt many straight people have begun to support us because of this argument — that we should not be discriminated against because our sexual orientation is genetic, or established too early. In any case, it's not a choice.

Growing evidence indicates that all sexual orientations apparently are not chosen. But let's face it, we still don't know what causes heterosexuality. Yet in the long term this popular, temporarily often politically effective argument, is disastrous both as a strategy for securing real equality and as a mark of personal self-acceptance.

First, it implies that the healthy, natural, even "God-given," standard really is the kind of culturally conditioned "straight heterosexuality" held up as normal. So being LGBT is a deviation, a genetic defect, like not being able-bodied.

From society, the most positive automatic response to this is: those poor dears, they can't help themselves. They're not really mainstream Americans like us. Let's pity them and help them overcome the limitations related to their homosexuality, which may include discrimination. We are "the straight man's burden."

And we are so desperate for acceptance by the dominant group, that this can feel wonderful. On the other hand, the most negative response might be to seek for the "gay gene" in order to correct it, prevent it, or abort it in the future.

Second, the response assumes that if people did have a free choice, they would choose to be "straight" as our society currently defines it. This is a basic assumption of heterosexism, the systematic belief that the conditioned heterosexual (the "straight") role (the straight role is conditioned, the heterosexual orientation is not) is the natural, healthy, norm.

However, people do not have a free choice — everything forces them, even if their orientation is not heterosexual, to seek conditioned heterosexuality, being straight.

Otherwise coming out would have been easy for everyone. But violence, threats, ridicule, humiliation, isolation, and rejection would have been the response of families, schools and peers if as teenagers we had announced our plans to love, date, and marry someone of the same sex.

And we heard that message very early.

In fact, that's what scares many who oppress LGBT people and believe that sexual orientation is a choice. They are really afraid that homoerotic lifestyles *are* more appealing and that, without the oppression, most people would choose them. No one has documented this fear better than Michael Bronski in *The Pleasure Principle: Sex, Backlash and the Struggle for Gay Freedom* (1998).

Third, the response that we had no choice deflects our gaze from the healing that our society really needs in order to overcome every oppression and the fear-based nature of our culture. It does not direct us to the heart of the matter — that the only reason people should be free from any oppression is it is important to honor love wherever it is found, no matter how fleeting, fragile, and inelegant it might be. It's important to love and to recognize the often awkward attempts of others to try to accept real love and to love in return.

Human health and hope require us to replace our entire fear-based way of thinking with one that is love-based. Many spiritual teachers who have graced this planet, proclaimed such a possibility and were oppressed for doing so.

But our fear-based society responds that only fear will work, not love. Without hell, it teaches us to believe, people will live like the devil. Talk of love is just plain naive.

This is the lie that makes all oppression seem inevitable, a lie that fuels the military-industrial-prison complex that increasingly dominates us. Should we begin to live on the basis of our real, inward connection to our planet and all life on it, we could not be sold the array of products that advertising convinces us will make us feel the closeness we already deeply have. Ironically, consumerism cannot bring the closeness it promises, for that closeness would end our need to buy more.

But the most important reason to stop responding that I wouldn't choose my orientation, is that saying I wouldn't be the way I am, I wouldn't be LGBT, if I had a choice, is internalized self-hate. It's like saying I wouldn't be a woman, or man, or "white," or a person of color, if I had a choice. It's the desire to flee something we are.

Health requires that we, ourselves, in our hearts, someday respond: "Yes, if I had a choice, I would be who I am, because being gay, lesbian, bisexual, or transgender is a gift. No matter what others say, no matter what the oppression, the homophobia, and what the heterosexist culture says, I am who I should be. I am at peace with myself, at home in my being, and determined to live in touch with all that I am."

The Real Tragedy of Turning Thirty

I admit I was somewhat amused when I heard a twenty-nine year old man at a bar genuinely bemoan the fact that he was about to turn thirty. The specter of that event looming over him, he said, made him "feel old." So, he told us, he needed to get some things done and find a partner before that happened — and while he "still had a chance."

To those of us who are quite a bit older, and who would never go back to thirty again, unless it was guaranteed that we could take with us all we have learned from our experiences since, there is something quite sad about feeling "old" at thirty.

I'm not sure what "feeling old" even means, and I don't think I do "feel old." But it's not meant positively. I know that's so, because we take the statements, "You don't look that old," or "You don't act that old," as complements.

Though this cult of youth is especially strong in gay male circles, it's just another one of those larger cultural values our conditioning has internalized in us. Idealizing youth enables our economic system to sell youthfulness to all of us by marketing cosmetics, cosmetic surgery, physical fitness, clothing styles, and a lot else. It even helps sell the chemicals that alleviate our depression over "feeling old."

We know what this does to those who are elders in our communities. They are shunted aside, taken less seriously, ignored, left out of our identities, stereotyped, and made the butt of jokes. Since LGBT communities focus on youth, our elders withdraw from our activities, deny us their experience, expertise, and support, and provide few visual models of what it could be like for those of us who are younger to "grow old" as LGBT people.

This is a tragedy for them. How many of the heroes of our liberation movement have disappeared because it is clear they are unwanted at the time when we need them most? They have heard too often that "old" means out-dated.

But this is also a tragedy for our youth, those like that twenty-nine year old who saw nothing positive about joining the ranks of those "over the hill" thirty-somethings.

Not only does it deny us all the history we need to define ourselves so that we can actively and effectively engage our culture and its prejudices against us. Not only does it deny us the voices of experience we need to develop the broader perspective on current events which only those who have been through similar events before can give us. Not only does it deny us those who can be our wise leaders, advisors, and mentors.

But it promotes the stereotypes of growing old, especially the oppressive stereotypes of the elderly male as someone who will somehow prey on youth. When our male elders do appear among youth, we have been taught to expect them to be "chicken hawks," or "dirty old men." And Patricia Nell Warren, of *Frontrunner* fame, and now over sixty, writes of older lesbians who are tired of "just being ignored" or made to feel unwelcome at women's events "where pheromones are in the air."

Most acutely in the gay male community, an ageist caste system seems to rule male social and sexual lives. Few older men are able to ignore the stigma of this blatant ageism in order to be seen among us. If they were to stay in touch, we could know that there is life — even vital, exciting, active, and fulfilling life — as we all age. We might begin to see that the life of our elders is even something to be desired.

It's no wonder that many young gay men see no future in their natural aging process. Not only have older gay people abandoned their old haunts and left them to youth, no longer dancing, laughing, playing pool, just hanging out, or stimulating the conversation. They have left us only with the stereotypes.

If it's only the negative stereotypical images of aging we experience, then, what future is there for those who are younger and must face the fact that they too are doomed to inevitably age? If all there is is youth, then why not devalue one's future? Why not think only of the present and expect all else to be down hill? Why not practice unsafe sex since there is nothing to look forward to anyway?

If it's bad to be old, then what does that do to the self-esteem of us all as every single one of us, without exception, inevitably moves to that wretched place? If it's that bad to age, then why not commit suicide when problems mount up now? It's not going to get any better than this youthful experience, we've been told.

We need a revolution in our thinking about age in order to have healthy youth. We need our elders with us in the places we live, work, and play. We need them to fight against our ageist prejudices with all the passion they have used to fight against homophobia.

We need to confront our deeply ingrained ideas of aging and prepare a healthy, positive strategy for our own aging. We'll have to talk with each other about how we feel about growing older. Somehow in order to save our youth we need to begin to celebrate our elders. We need to end the jokes, the stereotypes, and the put-downs. We need to consciously cross generations in all that we do.

It means all of us will have to confront the larger culture again. We'll have to really see that the American cult of youth is nothing but consumer mythology. And before we grow any older ourselves, even before we turn thirty, we need to embrace what Asian cultures embrace when they say, "There's nothing as beautiful as gray hair and a long beard."

The Psychological Debate is Over

We just can't seem to stop getting into arguments with people who plainly don't want to accept LGBT human beings. These people latch on to any straws that will keep them from admitting their own prejudices, fears, denial, and insecurities. Then they act out their personal problems on non-heterosexuals and heterosexuals who support basic LGBT rights.

Sincere seekers of understanding are reachable, but those who hold onto their biases for a variety of personal reasons continue to fish for any basis outside themselves that prevents their own growth and our progress. Using psychology in this way became even more popular in the last century. Today so-called psychological claims are the most often cited "scientific" arguments for supporting the idea that LGBT people are sick and need "conversion therapy" or "reparative therapy."

In response, we get caught up again and again arguing psychology with them. It's exhausting for us. It keeps us from more progress in our lives. And it prevents them from self-understanding and admitting that they're just prejudiced. Often we want to be "nice" about it, we don't want to offend, and we hope we can "help them understand."

We can call their prejudices "homophobia," searching for motives behind them, but the reality is, it's just plain denial. They won't face the fact that they are prejudiced, and we are often enabling them in this denial.

Let's be clear, then. What people who argue from psychology against LGBT people are doing is promoting, often in sincerity and in a successful money-raising fashion, a return to something like the Dark Ages of psychology and religion. Back then gay people were considered sick, perverted, inhuman, "the problem," and "unnatural."

On top of their use of religion, they deny their plain old bigotry by clinging to "scientific" language to legitimate their position. Their "experts" promote out-dated, unproven, and destructive theories that treat homosexuality as a psychological problem associated with such things as identification with the "wrong" parent or the "wrong" gender role. Their models of those they claim to have "converted" have their own problems. Who knows what they are?

But when will these anti-gay people get with it? How long will they hang on to their prejudices? How long will they accuse mainstream psychological professional groups of being the ones who are wrongly motivated?

How long must we listen to their ignorance? How long will we argue with them as if *we* are the ones who need to justify ourselves psychologically?

It's not that "ex-gay" leaders don't know that they are acting like enemies of science. They just refuse to change the prejudices upon which they've built their self-image.

In their attempts to convert, cure, or change sexual orientations that they don't like, they refuse to give up their lucrative strategies and recognize what all mainstream psychological organizations have been saying *for over 25 years*. Yes, that's a quarter of a century!

It wasn't just yesterday, but back in 1973 that the American Psychiatric Association's Board of Trustees confirmed that: "homosexuality does not meet the criteria to be considered a mental illness." Since then, *all* (yes, that's all) major professional mental health organizations have gone on record to affirm that homosexuality is *not* a mental illness.

Is that not clear enough? Listen to the unambiguous language of an American Psychiatric Association's statement about attempts to "convert, repair, or cure" homosexuality:

"The American Psychiatric Association opposes any psychiatric treatment, such as 'reparative' or 'conversion' therapy, which is based upon the assumption that homosexuality per se is a mental disorder, or based upon a prior assumption that the patient should change his/her homosexual orientation."

Yes, that does say "opposes." In fact, the APA says the "therapy" these anti-gay groups tout as loving is hardly positive for the patient: "The potential risks of reparative therapy are great: including depression, anxiety, and self-destructive behavior, since therapist alignment with societal prejudices against homosexuality may reinforce self-hatred already experienced by the patient."

There is just no debate here. The other professional psychological and medical organizations all agree — the American Psychological Association, the National Association of Social Workers, the American Counseling Association, the American Academy of Pediatrics.

Back in 1975, the American Psychological Association agreed with the American Psychiatric Association and made it clear that: "Homosexuality per se implies no impairment in judgment, stability, reliability, or general social and vocational capabilities."

And the stand of real psychological professionals on this issue is not just neutrality. Like the American Psychiatric Association, the American Psychological Association expects professionals to be involved in proactive change: "Further, the American Psychological Association urges all mental health professionals to take the lead in removing the stigma of mental illness that has long been associated with homosexual orientations."

In summary: "The American Psychological Association opposes portrayals of lesbian, gay, and bisexual youth and adults as mentally ill due to their sexual orientation and supports the dissemination of accurate information about sexual ordination, and mental health, and appropriate interventions in order to counteract bias that is based in ignorance or unfounded beliefs about sexual orientation."

Yes, the professional association says, "take the lead" in removing the prejudice. Yes, they say, "counteract the bias" toward gay people.

We must assume, then, that any so-called "therapists" who continue to promote prejudice and "cures," even those who merely don't stand up for LGBT people, are, frankly, acting unprofessionally. And we should say so.

We must assume, as the professionals themselves say, that counselors who disagree with established professional standards are promoting ignorance and bigotry. They somehow need to obsess with this issue in the same way that prejudice based on race or right-handedness refused to change no matter what the evidence.

And it's time we stopped arguing and said so. We don't need to be on the psychological defensive. We don't need to play into their game of responding to the same old claims they have made for years about issues that have been settled for decades. We don't need to answer their arguments with anything more than: "I know that people believe that, but it's unprofessional, so I don't."

The debate is over. We need to say that, repeat it, and act like it.

How Proud Are We Ready to Be?

Pride festivals are still important events in LGBT life, though we hear voices saying we are "post-pride" from people who are starting to feel and act mainstream. On the other end of the spectrum there are those who criticize pridefests as "just another party" when what we need, they say, is more political activism.

Though some of us think we've arrived and need these Pride parties no more, though some of us still don't want to "flaunt it" even though "straightness" is flaunted 24/7, though some of us seem to be apologetic for letting people know we are not heterosexual, and though some of us think partying and political activism are opposed, it looks as if we still need the public partying that pridefests represent. We still need to display pride in who we are as people who are not "straight."

That's certainly not what our enemies want, though. They prefer that publicly we look as if we are as miserable as they claim gay people, especially those living that "gay lifestyle" thing, really are. We're supposed to be completely depressed, lonely, incapable of loving, meek, ashamed, and on the verge of suicide because of our sexual orientation.

And it would suit their portrayal of us just fine if we who are happy would just hide in couples away from the public eye. Even we sometimes think that huddling away from it all is actually a sign of health.

They hate that we can have fun, that we enjoy being non-"straight." And the more they hate it, the more they are certifying that they themselves are as miserable as they often seem. A puritan, the not-so-tongue-in-cheek definition goes, is someone who is afraid that somewhere, somehow, someone might be having fun. This fear is more mainstream than we may have realized.

Those of us who object to more celebrations seem to have bought into the need for a life of "all misery all the time." It's true that there is much more to do to attain real equality and recognition of our full humanity by society. I object to those who act as if we've made it. They are out of touch with mainstream LGBT life.

But we need to get beyond any idea that we are non-heterosexual because we "couldn't help it" and celebrate the fact that we actually like ourselves enough so that if we did have a free choice in the matter, and no matter what others might think, we would choose who we have found ourselves to be. If we don't feel that way, it's not because we are LGBT. It's a sign that we need some good counseling and a support group so we can learn to like ourselves better.

Now, I think all human beings should be proud of their sexual orientations. They should be proud of who they're attracted to. They should be proud of their sex lives. They should be proud of their personal talents, characteristics, quirks, and gifts.

They should be proud of their accomplishments and achievements as long as they further the humanity of us all. I'm unconvinced that the ability to make money is one of them, however. If the goal of a company or person is just to increase wealth, rather than provide a service or product we really need, that doesn't seem to be much to be proud of.

Yet, I'm not sure what "straight pride" would look like, because I'm not convinced that "straight" is a healthy condition for human beings. I know that "straight" is not just being born heterosexual, because you have to relentlessly train people to act 'straight," heterosexual or not. "Straight" is just a role we are all expected to learn.

So, I suspect "straight pride" might be more like "white pride." It would define itself by what it is not — it's not like gay people, not queer, not freely creative, not free to be fully human; it's uptight and worried that it might look "queer" — and by what it's against — LGBT people and their love.

There is much for heterosexual people to be proud of, but it's not that they're "straight-acting," which takes no imagination. And as long as LGBT people are the scapegoats for straight-conforming people's poor self-concepts and their failure to be in touch with their own natural sexual orientation, we have evidence that heterosexuality has not come out from under its "straight" mask.

It's hard for LGBT people to see the unhealthy nature of "straight" because we've been trained to demean our different ways of being and to worship the "straight" role that burdens and limits even the dominant orientation. We've been victimized enough to believe that the majority is somehow right.

In reality, let me suggest, for I really believe this, LGBT people are more likely to be our culture's healers, pioneers, and models of emotional, spiritual, and human health. In other words, the reality is the exact opposite of what those who cherish and enforce "straight" think and preach.

If we have learned to embrace, celebrate, and cherish our sexual orientation as an alternative to the roles enforced by our profit-oriented, coping-oriented, addictive, restrictive, homophobic, sexually-confused, gender-rigid, racist, able-bodyist, fear-based society — a society that has run out of new ideas and uses religion as the last bastion of justification because nothing else is left — we can lead as role models of human health.

I know that for many of us this is a crazy idea. We have bought "straight" as our model for so long and we have come to hope that acting and looking straight will save us. But now it's time to proudly embrace who we are. We have taken the biggest leap already by coming out of the big, straight role. Our only problem is that we may be tempted to go back. After all, we don't want to look too "queer."

Yet, the eventual health of our society depends upon our ability to challenge its current roles. LGBT people are the ones who can do it, and we can do it if we know that we have a lot to be proud of, and a lot of pride to publicly celebrate.

Our Gay Myths

S anta Claus and the beginning of a new millennium — we've just celebrated both of these myths. We know there's no Santa Claus, but need him to keep our retail sales up. We know that the millennium doesn't really end until midnight next December 31. I don't know why we celebrated it a year early except that 2,000 is a round number and somehow feels right — that's what makes good myths, how they feel. Even though they're not real, we celebrate anyway.

There are other myths we believe and celebrate and, because we do, they affect how we think about ourselves and how we live our lives. In past columns we've looked at a few, but there are plenty. Here's a list to start with.

It's a myth that there is anything wrong with you that has to do with you being gay, lesbian, bisexual or transgender. All our struggles with relationships, personal matters, and the challenges they entail, as well as the negative patterns we act out, have to do with oppression, gender roles, and commonly experienced, unhealed personal hurts from our pasts.

It's a myth that LGBT people are deficient at loving, caring, partnering, fidelity, and commitment. We are actually good at all of these, and we exhibit the same problems with them as straight people because of what the culture has taught us all. We need the same therapy or support to overcome anything in our lives that we don't want there.

It's a myth that LGBT people are not homophobic. We carry all the straight conditioning from our culture that heterosexual people do about fear of closeness with the same sex. If we are in denial about this, or refuse to face it, we'll have problems with intimacy and closeness in our most important relationships.

It's a myth that we cannot be successful at long-term relationships. We only need support for them and the conviction to do what it takes personally to make our own lives ready to form healthy relationships.

It's a myth that there is a single LGBT community. We are many communities trying to accept and embrace our differences and work together to end what is hurting all of us — the discrimination, the intimidation, the fear, and the religious and legal bigotry.

It's a myth that drag shows are an effective challenge to cultural gender roles. I think they can be fun, sometimes entertaining, and sometimes well-meaning, but the shows haven't done a thing to effectively challenge the roles imposed by society. Though drag queens individually have been cultural prophets (think of Stonewall), drag entertainment remains a marginalized curiosity which at its heart feeds on gender roles. In some ways the shows have a lot in common with the old minstrel shows and the painted black faces of those white entertainers who played upon racial stereotypes. Drag shows even allow some to use drag to hide behind culturally created, exaggerated gender masks in order to act out and speak out of their own unhealed bitterness.

It's a myth that sex in itself is ever the real issue. Though the conservative religious principle may have been, "Sex is dirty, save it for the one you love," and though our society uses sex to focus our attention on ourselves and off of society's real problems, sex is a means of communicating numerous other things.

It can communicate whatever one wants to express by it, and it is the message that makes the difference. It can express love, hurt, anger, fear, fun, joy, closeness, loneliness, intimacy, distance, honesty, falsehood, playfulness, obligation, power issues, or any number of messages. We get to choose what we want our sexual activities to express.

It's a myth that LGBT liberation can make further and lasting progress without confronting its racism, sexism, and classism. We can portray ourselves all we want as people with an abundance of disposable income. We can charge our credit cards to the max. We can do everything it takes to rise up in the class structure and forget and criticize those we leave behind. But it will not end discrimination against gay people or heal our wounds. It will ultimately provide new closets for us to hide in instead of being "out" as human beings. It will also distance us from the others we need in our lives, gay or straight, to end the discrimination.

It's a myth that all religions have always condemned homosexuality. This is just historically untrue. In *every* major religious tradition there have been, and still are, movements both for and against LGBT people. Religions affirmed or rejected LGBT people depending on other cultural pressures existing at the time such as economics, class structures, gender roles, and dominant social institutions.

It's a myth that when we preach against and threaten people about AIDS it will change their minds about unsafe sex in the long term. This is a failed strategy of conservative preachers and politicians. It's easy to do from the vantage point of those who "know better" than the rest of us. Education is step one, but it only goes so far. Scolding as if there is hell, fire, and brimstone only distances the unsafe from our preachers.

Real changes in people's lifestyles require the more difficult task of working with them to convince them that their value and beauty as human beings is worth their lives. You can't do that from a bully pulpit, as an all-knowing father figure, or by looking down from above at those sinful, ignorant souls.

It's a myth that our salvation as LGBT people is in separating ourselves from the on-going struggle for human rights by huddling together away from it all. We all need safe places to recover, relax, melt in a lover's arms, and re-create. We need parties like the Millennium March on Washington. We also need to stop what is hurting all of us.

Huddling is a scared, victim strategy. Acting to end discrimination is a way to face our fears, take back our power, affirm our love, and assure those we love.

Those are some of our myths. You could list more, but let's also get on with celebrating who we really are before the millennium truly ends.

We Don't Need a New Year to Change Our Lives

Another year is coming to an end. This time people will also celebrate the end of a millennium. These are just artificial markers of the movement of time, meaningless in the natural scheme of things. We humans give them any meaning and power they have.

For the rest of nature, December 31 merely is one day followed by another which may be no different from the day before. The sun will shine slightly longer on the northern hemisphere on January 1, 2000, than the previous day, but nature sees little more significance in one day or the other.

Why does this calendar mean so much to us, a calendar created by the Church to mark the religious seasons in sync with the holidays of pre-Christian civilizations? I have heard people answer with the belief that a new year is their real chance for new beginnings. It's as if this date is the only time to start anew, to change one's direction and to leave the past. It's as if it's the calendar that enables us to make the changes we want in our life. More often new year's resolutions fade first in practice and then in memory.

Calendars are not what change us. Our decisions to change are what make the difference, and we can make them without regard for time, day, or year. We are powerful enough to decide to be what we want to be. We take back this power by the decisions we make.

We are not victims who cannot feel good about ourselves without the approval of others. We can decide to think, to act, and to make decisions, based upon the belief that we lesbians, gay men, and bisexual and transgender people are whole, complete, valuable, and powerful.

We can make these decisions without the approval of anyone else. When we find ourselves not following through on our
decisions, we can remake them without blame or shame. We
can do so again and again till we have found our life's stride
which moves us as whole human beings into healthy relationships.

We can decide to create safe places to be who we are. We
can decide to never again settle for anything less than absolutely everything.

We can decide not to settle for girlfriends or boyfriends
who do not support our growth and are not willing and secure
enough to walk beside us on our paths with acceptance and
love.

We can decide to believe that love is not a limited commod-
ity and to reject the idea that if I love you it will diminish my
love for my friends, because in reality deep love between two
people spills over to change the world and everyone around
them.

We can decide to no longer accept the messages that all
good things must come to an end, or that the happiness I'm
feeling is too good to be true, or that romance never lasts, or
that there will be payback for any good I experience now.

We can decide that we are worth being loved and that it
is worth our own time to wait for a partner who will love us
for who we are and who we want to become. We don't have to
settle.

We can choose to be intimate with someone emotionally
and to be vulnerable with our feelings, hurts, and dreams with
someone we choose.

We can choose to set our own boundaries with those who
want to impose their negativity on us.

We can choose to act or not act on our emotions.

We can choose friends who support us. We can say goodbye to those who don't.

We can judge our own behavior, thoughts, and emotions, and take responsibility for them.

We can choose to offer no reasons or excuses for justifying our behavior. We can choose to say "I don't know," "I don't care," or "No," without feeling guilty. We can choose to say "I don't understand," without feeling stupid.

We can choose to be illogical in making decisions.

We can choose not to be responsible for finding solutions to other people's problems.

We can choose to change our minds.

We can choose to be independent of the good will of others before we choose to cope with them.

We can choose to organize and lead movements to end what is hurting us and our LGBT communities.

We can choose to do every small act that makes this world safer.

We can choose not to put off the happiness of holding our lover's hand, or kissing them goodbye, until the world accepts it. We can choose to ignore how others react while still taking care of our safety.

We can choose to recognize where we are afraid and distinguish it from what is really scary "out there." We can choose how much fear is worth to us and how it will change our actions.

Our decision making power is greater than we think. And when we make these choices we can also choose to feel how it feels again to live our lives by our own decisions. For many of us, that in itself might feel scary.

As children we learned that we had to live by the decisions of the adults around us. We may have been told that making our own decisions was selfish or stupid. As adults we no longer have to live with that message.

And we never have to wait for the right time of year to begin again, to re-decide, and to face the useless messages inside us that keep us from living as who we were made to be — the loving, caring, powerful, special LGBT people who provide the spice of life day after day after day and who stir up those who have never dreamt in their own lives that anyone could be so powerful and free.

Coming Out

The Minor Details

Coming Out and Staying In

I like the basic idea behind National Coming Out Day each October. I wish everyone whose sexual orientation is not the dominant one would just "come out."

I wish they could do so because our society was healthy enough about sex and sexuality to accept people who are gay, lesbian, bisexual, transgender, uncertain, or confused.

There doesn't seem to be a category for the confused and uncertain though. I also wish everyone believed that it was okay not to know for sure.

Even gay men and lesbians are suspicious about "what's really going on" with people who just might not know yet, or who are "experimenting." I suspect that if our society were healthier, we could accept that there are a lot more of these people than we want to admit. The uncertain and unsure could "come out."

National Coming Out Day should also be a time for us to give some people a break. Gay people have had enough guilt piled on them by society anyway, without LGBT communities adding another layer for not coming out.

Actually, appeals to come out are often quite classist. It's generally easier to be out in middle or upper class circumstances, than it is in working class environments.

As long as there is classism — including classism in our movements — other victimized groups, such as working class people, will find it easier to scapegoat LGBT people than to fight the all-pervasive structure of class in our society that effects us all. And as long as our dominant LGBT images are classist because they portray us with lots of disposable income, living in condos, high rises, and perfectly appointed homes, and having all the latest techno-gadgets, few working class people (gay or straight) will feel comfortable enough to join us as out.

It's just insensitive for someone who has little to lose by being out in her or his occupation to criticize a factory worker because she or he isn't ready to come out. That worker may have almost everything to lose.

If you're not out, come out only for the right reasons. Don't come out for just any reason that other "out" people will give you. And if you feel guilty about not coming out, then stay in until you have a better reason to come out than alleviating your guilt.

Some people want everyone to come out so they can be certain about who really is LGBT. It would make it easier for them to see potential dates, to pick people up, and just to decide how to act with others. That's not a good reason for you to come out.

Some people say we should come out because if everyone came out, the reality of those numbers would change the world. It's true that if everyone came out, it *would* change the world, but that's still not a good reason to come out. We who give such reasons, need to face the fact that we are really telling others to come out so we ourselves will feel better, or we will have a better life in some way, or we'll be safer because there is safety in numbers.

If you're in, then, don't come out to help the rest of us or to make other LGBT people feel better. Those aren't good reasons. It would keep those of us who are out from facing and dealing with the issues of life we really need to tackle. Instead of dealing with our real emotional issues, or instead of fighting our fight, we are acting as if *your* coming out is *our* solution.

Some have said we should come out because it will help heterosexuals get over their prejudices. They'll see the number and variety of LGBT people who are already in their lives. They'll see that we're "normal" people (I think that means that we're "straight-acting.").

This isn't a good reason either. No LGBT person owes the straight community anything around this issue. They owe us. So, whatever you do, don't come out to help anyone else.

There's only one good reason to come out. Come out for your own integrity and because you love yourself.

There's only one good time to come out. Come out only when *you* decide that *you* are ready. Don't come out one moment before that.

The act of coming out should be an act of power and self-love. It will change many things, but mostly, and most importantly, it will change you.

Remember, it's natural to be afraid. Change can feel very scary. And not just for you.

When you come out, some people may leave you and others will not. Some people will need a lot of time to rethink and re-feel how they are to be. Some will need to be reassured that they will not lose anything they value in your relationship with them. Others, will say, "Oh we thought so." Some might reject you. Others may love you for it.

There's no better book about coming out than Rob Eichberg's *Coming Out: An Act of Love* (1990). I suggest that you read it first, whether you're ready to come out or not. Then, begin the process called "coming out" only when you decide you're ready. As Eichberg says: "Coming out is a process of growth and learning; coming out proudly is a statement of one's strength and integrity."

In the meantime, whatever you decide, be gentle with yourself. And don't worry. When you're ready to leave the closet, you will.

Is Ricky or Isn't He?
We've Just Got to Know

Is it just curiosity born of boredom with one's own life — like speculating whether just anyone of any occupation, shape, or look that's standing in front of me in an unmoving line is or isn't — that has gay men wondering if singer Ricky Martin is gay or not? . . . And usually answering, he must be?

A recent cover story in *The Advocate*, which will probably qualify for one of its ten longest stories of the decade, certainly must prove that this is an important issue. And, as one of our national glossies that lets us all know what the latest trends are that we might otherwise be missing, does this mean I'm supposed to be dwelling upon this issue too?

The supermarket tabloids have been, but they haven't set the direction for my obsessions in the past. Or, are we already obsessed with this question? So, Ricky on a cover would just be a marketing tactic to sell more magazines to gay men?

And what difference will it make? Will it stop the latest ballot initiatives and legislation from appearing that will deny lesbians, gay men, and bisexual and transgender people their equality? Will it add a couple of bucks to our organizations, or even my wallet? Why does this matter to me and to my community?

Does he fit a stereotype that we heavily promote, of someone who dresses in the latest gay man's drag? Must he be gay because he could fit right in at one of our stand and model bars, or one of our high energy dance clubs? Certainly his music seems to, but is he cute enough, thin enough, smooth enough, buffed enough, young enough, dressed well enough?

And what *is* in now for this segment of the gay consumer scene, anyway? I remember when it was Levis, then Guess, then Tommy wear? Is it plaid shirts with white tees under them, still? Or is it the collarless v-necks with the horizontal stripe? Is it even jeans at all, or is it tan Dockers? Help me, glossies, to know!

And the haircut, is it short enough? So many things to keep track of as we spend our money on looking the part so we'll be found, or find someone who is attracted to us for the look, or create an armor of clothing and cosmetics that doesn't let people see how we may really be hurting, or scared, or confused, or lonely.

Is the fact that he fits the current look of the young, gay consumer the clue to our interest?

Or do we want him to be gay because we want to surround ourselves with as many celebrities who are "like us" as possible? Is it the safety of numbers, especially the number of celebrities? These are people who the populace likes; and, if they like him, and he's gay, maybe, just maybe, they'll like us better. And maybe he'll finally come out and speak for us. Celebrity voices are so much more important than our own.

There is safety in numbers, of course, but we will always be a small minority that needs to attain equality and keep it. Every non-dominant group knows that the struggle continues. Look at the turning back of affirmative action in the past decade out of misdirected white fear that the real cause of their problems is advantages for people of color.

Though there may be safety, and a temporary sense of not feeling so different, numbers will not provide self-acceptance and self-love. Otherwise we would see more heterosexual people who love themselves enough not to scapegoat us for their insecurities. No, Ricky can't provide self-acceptance for us.

Or is this similar to our obsession with finding gay people everywhere we can in history? Of course they are there, and they have been hidden by the dominant histories. But we sure do like to rush to pronounce the judgement that any man who shows closeness to another man must have been gay, or any woman who is close to another woman must be a lesbian. Was Abe Lincoln, or wasn't he, after all? Why does it matter?

That's our internalized homophobia in the form of believing that no one can be heterosexual who is close to their own sex. And that reinforces the reason why gay men, lesbians, and bisexual and transgender people are discriminated against — to keep all human beings from getting close to their own sex by the "evil" gay rumor. If two men are close, it goes, they must be having sex, because men can only express closeness through sex.

This reflects mainstream male conditioning around sex, but it's not who males really are. Sex is great, no doubt, but there are hundreds of ways to express closeness to another human being of the same sex, another sex, or of ambiguous sex. And we wouldn't promote that view of men, would we?

So, that can't be the reason we want Ricky to be gay, can it?

Maybe, then, it's some or all of the above, and more than just a passing curiosity.

If it's more, our needs won't let us put the issue away. We'll join the tabloids because we need to do so. And our community will hound Ricky Martin with the question.

That's a really unsupportive way to treat another human being who actually may be struggling with issues of sexual orientation and has a right to do so. We of all people should empathize with such struggles.

Or, we could accept him either way, for his music, his talent, or his stage presence, and then his orientation won't matter to us. Don't we tell straight people that orientation shouldn't matter?

When I first found *The Advocate* article in a coffee shop, I didn't read it myself. So, I really don't know what the answer is. But the man next to me, who let me know that he was gay, was absorbed in it. After reading the expose, he concluded that he still didn't know about Ricky. "But," he added, "he must be."

Growing Up in the USA

The Minor Details

Don't Let School Dumb You Down

John Taylor Gatto was named New York State Teacher of the Year in 1991. This author of the book *Dumbing Us Down* (1991) observed in an interview, "My license certifies me as an instructor of English language and literature, but that isn't what I do at all. What I teach is school, and I win awards doing it."

Right-wing think tanks continue to promote the misrepresentation of the over-all, measurable success of America's public educational system in terms of its limited failures, and the media repeat these misrepresentations. So, at first we might think that Gatto's is just another conservative critique meant to prepare the populace for accepting school vouchers and government aid to parochial schools.

It's not. He's telling us that our schools, both public and private, have a basic agenda that stifles our inborn humanity, and he's doing something about it.

As I understand it, this is because American schools (educator John Dewey called our public schools the "churches" of America) are meant to teach us to be "good citizens." That means, first and foremost, that we are taught to become governable. We are taught to be in awe of the powers in our society, to respect them, and to do nothing that subverts the dominant paradigm. It means we are taught to subordinate our own ideas, creativity, and intuitions to the ones that will keep us from changing things, and those in power, too radically.

In the past, our schools have helped instill the prejudices of race and ethnicity, and on the whole they still teach classism, able-bodyism, heterosexism, and homophobia, as well as a less-conscious racism. Anyone who points this out will be considered suspect, overly negative, subversive, leftist, un-American, etc.

It's okay to criticize our schools for failures related to not providing business with the kinds of workers, managers, and consumers corporate America needs. It's not okay to criticize them for failing to produce human beings who are in touch with their inborn humanity and intrinsic, personal worth.

As the second part of being good citizens, schools teach us to be good consumers. That doesn't mean teaching us the values of simplicity, of love based upon our inherent connection to all life on the planet, and the value of individuals in all their complicated and challenging diversity. It means preparing us to make more money so we can consume more, spend more, buy our worth, show our consumption to others, and be better than others without having to say so — our toys, cars, and homes should make it so obvious that we don't have to say a word.

Third, it means that we are taught to be competitive. Seldom questioned today is the dogma that competition with others is healthy and good. It's what gives us all the *things* we have today. We are taught to be in competition (sometimes even labelled "healthy" competition) with others and the planet. To challenge that idea is to be suspect too.

Fourth, since the major justification Americans give for an education is that it will get you a "better" job, our schools teach us not only that we will have to compete with all life forms for a limited number of "good" jobs, but that the economic standard of more money equates with the moral standard of "good." After all, those people must be good, we come to believe; they've got a good credit-rating.

These ideas are usually unexamined, but some teachers try to raise these issues, try to counteract the ideas in the face of the overwhelming messages to consume, conform, and earn one's personal worth. John Gatto is one.

Students in LGBT communities need to examine these issues themselves when they face school again. We all need to ask how much we want to assimilate to these standards, and why.

When one finally accepts that most difficult realization that one stands outside the dominant sexual orientation, and faces the consequences of that "queerness," a new freedom opens. They can stand outside all the dominant standards and examine them to decide what it could be like to live our own lives on our own terms with the others we choose to include in our life.

Those who have embraced this freedom have led progressive movements for change, produced great art, challenged the limits cultures place on creativity, refused to be stifled by gender roles, broken the sick fears of the dominant culture around sex and pleasure, and defined life in whole new terms. We LGBT people do have important gifts to give to our culture that will shake it up for all humanity's sake if we don't hide.

Yet the dominant teachings tell us it's better to blend in, to accept all the other rules of this game our culture plays, so that we can be tolerated as gay people. If that is the path we accept — and many of our own political leaders tell us to do so — we may be able to blend into the woodwork. But we'll have lost the opportunity to give the kind of gifts to our culture that other non-dominant groups have given when the dominant culture "discovered" their art, music, tastes, ideas, ways of thinking, and human variety, as contributions to diversity.

No matter how our educational system wants us to blend in, we can choose either to take that easy, well-worn path or we can face our fears, live our lives fully, and contribute to deep rooted change in a world that needs people who live outside the same old, worn-out ideas and answers to human problems. The only difference today is that old ideas and answers are dressed up in the clothing of cyber-drag.

Real living begins with all the little challenges that everyday life raises, and continues until the world is a better place for all life. And we get to choose to so live: taking from our educational careers what helps us thrive in life while refusing to be "dumbed down" by any institutions.

Our culture needs such refreshing people.

Sports Culture:
Boys on the Playground

If you were a boy, you know that at some point playground culture became sports culture. If you were able to master and enjoy the first, that didn't always mean you could succeed at the second. Play moved into competition as early as society could get us to internalize the idea that we were vying with other boys for affirmation and the emblem of "manhood."

The boys who were "real boys" (those who were most likely to grow up to be "real men") were the best at competitive play. They were "winners." They were the ones who most successfully internalized the competitive spirit that our culture needs to keep its economy and military going.

Internalizing that model of manhood is how most of us actually came to believe that "competition is good." And we've built a society so dependent upon competition that it's hard to even think about how we could live well without it.

It's one of those unquestioned basic truths men and women are supposed to accept as they both value manhood, even if what competition is good for is not human relationships but production and profits. It's sure "good for business." It can produce lower prices and cheaper goods, more sales and faster computers, larger portfolios and bigger empires. Its current cost, however, is our humanity.

On top of all that, a competitive attitude toward others is a key ingredient in homophobia. It keeps us separate. And competition between men keeps them unconnected and fighting with each other at the other man's expense in order to get society's "rewards."

Male sports are one place we learn all this. We also learn who the "losers" are. If we didn't master sports' skills, we not only were left out, but were picked on by the other boys. If we couldn't throw a spiral pass if our life depended on it, stood in right field praying that no one would hit the baseball there, didn't want to punch or get punched, or threw a ball "like a girl," we were the targets of this "manhood." If we were the youngest, smallest, thinnest, heaviest, or most gentle and caring boy in the class, we could expect "fag" jokes from the other boys.

It could have started even before the sports culture hit. The elementary school playground usually had bullies who lived out their insecurities on the smaller boys. It was full of boys who had internalized masculinity's "beat or be beaten" requirement for acceptance. In most cases, the boy who tried to remain in touch with his full humanity was just out of luck.

And if you also began to realize that you "liked" boys, that you fantasized about them, especially the ones who fit the culture's model of the "real man," confusion was added to fear. Whatever those feelings meant (and who was there to explain them?), they set a boy apart even further from the ideal man.

In reality we were all afraid of each other on that playground. Some of us remember the fear. Others buried the fear under the role of the bully or sports star, or by staying inside and mastering the subjects of the mind, such as reading and math. Fortunately, the mental world and its own competition would somewhat begin to replace physical accomplishments as we entered the "grown-up" world of men, even if it never fully removed the manhood lessons of the playground.

Of course, "real men" can't admit such fear, even to themselves. But it was there. And it's still there on athletic teams at all levels. It promotes the homophobia and the gay bashing that continues in most sporting venues.

I'm convinced that the level of competition in sports today requires homophobia. Teamwork for men means the ability of one group of men to band together to beat, defeat, or kill other men, whether that's on the athletic field, on the battlefield, or in business or politics.

And true winning as currently defined is always at another man's expense. This means that though we are "improving" the "level" and opportunities for women's athletics, they must be kept separate from male activities. "Beating a girl" is an insult for "real men," not an accomplishment.

I am not talking about play, but sports. Play is free, fun, a letting go of oneself and one's ego. It's the child-like activity that doesn't concentrate on techniques, talents, abilities, performance and the evaluations of others. It gets caught up in light-hearted, "unproductive" fun.

But how often do we begin a game in play and realize that we've flipped into the issue of winning and losing, of "beating" the other person. That's the conditioning.

Sports are the opposite of play today. They are either the big business of college and professional athletics or they are farm leagues for younger children which provide competition for future players on the "next level."

And they need homophobia, the fear of getting close to your own sex. You just can't treat people this way and be really close.

This attitude is carried over into our most intimate relationships. Play is the key to good sex, not techniques, talents, and comparisons and competition. Play takes place when we're comfortable with ourselves. And it's childlike. But everything in our society tries to take that out of us, and the hurts of the playground and the demands of our athletic system are part of what changed us to keep us from playing and connecting on a real human level.

The boy who was "left out" because he didn't fit was the one most in touch with his humanity. He was also most aware that sports culture was trying to tear his humanity from him to prepare him for what our fear-driven society, not human beings, needed.

If that boy could have been able to fight all that, he would have been the one on the playground with real courage, the real hero. Often he did fight as long as he could, against all the odds.

Sports Culture:
Girls on the Playground

J ust look at her. There's something so free about the girl
on the playground who hasn't gotten the message that she
should act like a "little lady." The playground is her place to
soar, to dream of flying, driving a race car, climbing mountains,
becoming a great soccer star, or setting new records on the
basketball court.

She can get dirty, tear her jeans, scrape her elbows and
shins, hang upside down forever, shout and laugh uncontrol-
lably, and make any sound from any body part that she wants.
For a time in her life, there are no limits placed on her just
because she's a girl.

She thinks of her body in terms of how it functions to
accomplish her many dreams, not as an object judged by others. She couldn't care less about how she looks and what she
wears as long as it helps her to run fast and jump high or do
whatever else she wants to do.

She might be called a "tomboy," but that's not so bad in our
culture. Our society's sexism actually protects her for awhile. A
"girly boy" is of concern because we take boys more seriously
than girls. "Tomboys" are just different and cute the way little
children can be cute. We don't think of girls as that important
or that threatening. So, for a while she can ignore the system
and play.

Most girls have already gotten the message that they should
be preparing for, and thinking of themselves in terms of, what
boys want in a girl. It starts earlier than ever as our consumer
society sells little girls on how to be pretty, little ladies who
will attract boys. Dolls and television, even Mattel's "Barbie
Computer" (only $599) will tell them that their ultimate goal
will soon be to "get a man." That should be the real measure of

their success at femininity. And the sooner they prepare for it, the better.

At least by adolescence, the message becomes very clear. Be polite rather than honest. Be pretty rather than fun. Be quiet rather than look intelligent. Be deferential and dependent. Never compete with boys. Finally, forget that relaxed attitude toward your body and take up the self-criticism necessary to turn it into the image it should be to attract the attention and approval of men.

The girl who refuses to change and defer, to hide her self, or to sit quietly, will be criticized. She'll probably hear: "You'll never get a man that way." And if, frankly, she isn't interested in boys at all and continues in adolescence to be free from the pressures to look "straight," she may also maintain her freedom to accomplish what the "straight" and "straight-acting" girls are less likely to accomplish.

The girl who shows no interest in boys is free to remain her own active, rambunctious self, free to explore her athletic abilities, free to think of her body as hers and to push it to learn how few limits she actually has. As she does so, she'll be accused of being a lesbian. And as long as that's considered a bad thing, the lesbian slur will be an effective tool to put most women back into the role of a dependent lady.

The pressures to become "ladylike" are everywhere, strong, and confusing. They may tear the young woman up inside as she struggles with the fact that her own dreams are being ripped from her to squeeze her into a gender role.

However, if she continues not to care at all, or if she finds that her sexual and erotic orientation is for other women and can live with that, she's more free to pursue her athletic dreams than the girl who sets her sights on getting a man. We are more likely to find her on athletic teams, or at the top of the class academically. In spite of the odds, she has courageously broken the rules.

In athletics she can find a protective space in which to grow. As psychologist Mary Pipher points out in the now classic book *Reviving Ophelia* (1991), girls in sports are often more emotionally healthy than those who are not. They are a member of a peer group that defines its members by their own abilities rather than popularity, wealth, boyfriends, or beauty. They can choose their own self-discipline and athletic goals, and can cooperate with other girls. They can bond with other women for a cause. And they can do so without males.

Even with the rise of successful women in sports, there remain attempts to make sure women defer to men. It's not just the past preponderance of male coaches. Women's sports have been devalued. Only with the Federal Title Nine Program has equality been possible. And that federal program (Note all the conservative politicians who continue to be against "the feds" interfering with education.) is probably most responsible for the fact that the United States has a world championship women's soccer team.

Yet, the put-down that women with great athletic abilities are lesbians remains. In effect it says they're not "real women."

As long as culture considers it bad for a woman to be a lesbian, that accusation will be an effective method of controlling women. And lesbians will be represented out of proportion to their numbers on athletic teams.

It's not that lesbians have more inherent athletic ability than heterosexual women. It's just that they have often been more free to stay in touch with that ability. They do not need to be defined by men.

Until society changes its attitude toward lesbians, that'll be the case. In the meantime, it will take courageous women who do not "need" men to make women's sports great.

A number of years ago I was called in to help in response to a report that a male women's athletic coach had announced to his college team that: "There will be no lesbians on this team."

It was unquestionably a discriminatory remark and had to be dealt with institutionally. But given the realities of the pressures on most women today to stifle their talents, my first response was, "Doesn't he want to win at all?"

What Have We Been Doing to Our Children?

"Poisonous pedagogy." That's what world-renowned Swiss psychotherapist Alice Miller calls our current dominant methods of child-rearing. It's a hard label to swallow. We'd rather deny it. But she's dead serious.

Miller's writings are extensive and important, including her most well-known book, *The Drama of the Gifted Child: The Search for the True Self* (1979), or *For Your Own Good: Hidden Cruelty in Child-rearing and the Roots of Violence* (1990), and *Thou Shalt Not Be Aware: Society's Betrayal of the Child* (1998). In every one she challenges much of what we consider "normal" parenting.

Miller calls for a total revision of the methods we use and the way we view children. She describes how parents, who haven't dealt with the effects of the poisonous pedagogy of their own parents, project their ideas, feelings, and dreams on their children. Children learn that in order to survive they must honor and obey their parents while repressing memories, feelings, and attempts to be themselves. Children must learn to conform, suppress their curiosity and emotions, and become intolerant, even afraid, of deviations from what they've learned.

This parenting, we sincerely believe, is "for their own good." In order not to face the pains, humiliations, disappointments, tragedies, and abuses of our own up-bringing, we won't look deeply at the issue. In fact, we refuse to take our own childhood feelings and experiences seriously.

As a result we've become unaware of what really happened. We're convinced that anything we went through was good for us, character-building, or necessary training to get along in the real world. "My childhood wasn't that bad." "I turned out okay," we respond, even if our childhood was frankly abusive.

In addition, our culture still tends to teach children to blame themselves as if adults are innocent and children born guilty. As the magnitude and variety of child abuse in our culture continues to come to the surface, we just don't want to face it.

We learn to defend our parents and blame ourselves for any negative things they've done and for our inabilities to rise above them. We want to protect parents. We want to let them off the hook. We want to say they were well-meaning, even if they were screwed-up. We want to tell adult children that they should forgive their parents. And the worst commandment, the one used to support the illusion that parenting is just fine and children need to get over it, Miller adds, is "Honor your father and your mother."

So, as adults we deal with depression, surprising amounts of anger, self-defeating internal messages, low self-esteem, and patterns of actions through which we constantly attempt to prove we're really not stupid, insignificant, abandoned, unlovable, or worthless.

We're still not supposed to add to "Well my parents did the best they could (given their own upbringing)," the realization that they were incapable of giving us what we needed as children. Parents so needed their children to fulfill their own unmet childhood needs that they couldn't love them unconditionally, couldn't let them grow in their own ways, couldn't always fully be there, couldn't take children's feelings seriously, or couldn't affirm, respect, and believe their children.

When children learn to suppress their feelings, they learn not to feel much of what's really going on around them. They often become violent.

It's not about violence on TV. Children who have really been loved and protected, Miller asserts, are uninterested in violent movies and video games. The child who was hurt and humiliated, maybe not by parents but at school, will seek an object to hate and on which to take revenge. The abuser was always abused. Violent people were brought up violently. And often they were also taught to deny their histories. These memories are unbearably painful. So one way not to feel the pain of childhood is to hurt or kill innocent people.

This is not to blame parents. They don't get much help either. The mainstream thinks this is the way it should be as long as parents don't go to extremes. It doesn't take alternative ideas seriously. It just doesn't want to face the hurts most of us felt as children. Parents are left to pass along the methods of their parents, though they often do improve them somewhat. And fixing this through permissiveness will not be the answer either.

Parents are given little support. They're taught to rely on an inadequate consumer-driven nuclear family model that's guaranteed to exhaust them. They're told to discipline children by hitting, yelling at, and humiliating them.

But Miller is blunt. Experiments, she says, have proven conclusively that no one learns anything from punishment. They only learn how to avoid more punishment through lies, pretense, and diversion. They also learn how to punish a child later.

Little children are naturally tolerant. They think it's wrong to be hurt. It makes sense to them that people who are hurting or left out should be helped. They have a sense of fairness. They don't object to showing affection to others of either sex. They expect human beings to cry out when they're in need. They look intently at others until they're told not to stare. They expect the best of other humans until they're taught not to trust. They laugh more, cry more, observe more, and dream more. They do things that are inefficient, unproductive, outside of the box. The world is theirs for exploring and loving.

Children are not naturally homophobic. They don't naturally think that sexuality is dirty. They aren't naturally racist. They have to be taught these things.

Childishness, of course, ends. We call it growing up. And it seems to be ending sooner than ever as we push younger and younger children to be like us adults — the adults who seek more and more external fulfillment, use addictive coping mechanisms, are unhappy with their looks, and buy books to improve their self-esteem and the many things they don't like about themselves. When children enforce on each other the prejudices and inadequacies they were taught by grown-ups, we call it peer pressure.

Not surprisingly, this poisonous pedagogy installs and enforces homophobia and prejudice against LGBT people. As generation after generation moves away from its methods, we'll slowly also move away from the search for others to blame for society's problems.

Still, there will be some who won't face the deep personal hurts from their parents' pedagogy. They couldn't bear to tell the truth about their parents. They may be psychologists, right-wing evangelists, anti-gay leaders, or others who prefer to blame LGBT people. They say, "I was hit, hurt, etc. and I turned out okay." Anti-gay efforts are less painful to them than feeling the pains of their childhood.

There is probably no anti-gay person who has fully faced their own up-bringing. And one way to avoid doing so is to focus hate, prejudice, arrogance, and disgust on LGBT people.

So, if Alice Miller's right, that's what their problem is. It's not us. It's their own inability to face their childhoods. The reality is, these people really need therapy.

Women, Men, and Gender

The Minor Details

We Need Transgender People
Out Proudly Among Us

There is something extremely important for gay men, lesbians, and bisexual people in the fight for the rights of transgender people. Yet, it has taken a long time for some of us to see this. And others still don't.

Transgender people embody the real issue behind the oppression of sexual minorities. To miss this point is actually to buy into the excuses the system itself gives for discriminating against and abusing non-heterosexual people.

The dominant excuse is that LGBT people are erotically attracted to the same sex. So, the system teaches that all of this has to do with who is having sex with whom or who is in love with whom.

We might think that's obviously true, but it's not really the case. One of the common dynamics of any oppression is that lies are convincingly repeated about the reasons for oppressing a victimized group. The system's excuses are never the real reasons.

White racism claims that the reason for the oppression of people of color is something inherent in "them" — their skin color, culture, or natural abilities. In reality, racism functions to keep working-class people apart, blaming and scapegoating each other so they'll never unite to end what is collectively hurting them in the culture and its institutions. It's a way of protecting the system itself. Martin Luther King, Jr. understood this and that's why he turned to challenging the whole system, not just personal prejudices.

Yet it's easy for a victimized group to believe those lies consciously or unconsciously and to think that on that basis they can correct something they're doing in order to end the oppression. In LGBT communities this means that we should try to look and act straight, particularly in public. We should never do anything to show that we are attracted to the same sex unless it's part of excusing ourselves with, "We're just like you, except...." That means we should treat our sexuality in the same sick manner straight people do.

When we recognize what's really going on when LGBT people are victimized and encouraged to think of themselves as second-class citizens, we'll see that we need a different strategy for our own liberation, one that includes and highlights transgender people. But it's a strategy far from that of many of us who think that straight, genderized people are healthy, and that how they live their lives and what they possess will be our salvation.

The real reason LGBT people are targeted for discrimination is that the oppression is the major means our society uses to keep men and women in their place, to keep them in strictly defined and "opposite" gender roles. It ensures that men will be "masculine" and women will be "feminine."

If any two self-identified heterosexual males walk down a street in the U.S. and hold hands or put their arms around each other, they'll be treated the way gay men are with violence, threats, ridicule, and rejection. That's because by doing so they have defied the male role. They have stepped out of the straight-jacket of masculinity. They have transcended the limits of their culturally-defined gender.

If a self-identified heterosexual woman refuses to follow male concepts of female beauty, refuses to find her sole worth in approval and acceptance by men, stands up with her sisters for equal pay for equal work, and decides to live her life in her own self-interest (as only men are supposed to), she will be accused of being a lesbian. She too has transcended the stifling gender role society has for her.

As long as we have gender defined as we do, men will be stuck in their place, out of touch with their feelings of hurt, fear, and confusion, and living the "beat or be beaten" mentality with other men they learned in childhood. It's a role enforced with the "privilege" men are taught they have: the privilege of defending this system by being willing to kill other men and be killed by them in the name of manliness. If they don't, they will be treated as "non-masculine" males, as gay men.

As long as we have gender defined the way we do, the limitations on women will remain. They'll be suspect for acting powerful, assertive, decisive, and feminist. They'll be put down for showing anger, reason, and clarity of thought and goals, for finding fulfillment in their own wholeness, for deciding how they want to look and act, and for no longer believing that "getting a man" is the key measure of their worth.

As long as gender is strictly defined and enforced with little if any fluidity, gay men and lesbians will be attacked, demeaned, and thought of as second class citizens because the oppression has nothing to do with them and everything to do with gender roles — roles that are not human, freely chosen, or healthy. These roles result in inhuman relationships: one role relating to another rather than one human being relating to another.

Transgender people embody our real issue. Their "coming out" threatens the entire system of gender identity and gender roles. Their presence announces boldly and openly that none of us "has to be" either of these roles. And that's a major threat to everything that oppresses us. Suzanne Pharr was absolutely right when she wrote *Homophobia: A Weapon of Sexism*, now in its second edition (Chardon, 1997). And I would put it, "Homophobia: A Weapon of Gender Rigidity."

Society's fear is that if we take away the two gender roles we will not know who we are. In reality, we'll get in touch with our unconditioned, free humanity by rejecting externally imposed, dysfunctional, and inhuman, definitions of what it is to be human, male and female. That fear — that without the roles I won't know who I am — might be the scariest of all. Yet, it opens us up to one of the most exciting frontiers of exploration in the universe: the exploration of all that we can be.

We will not be free until transgender people of all types can define who they are and how they want to express their self-chosen identities. It's not really about sexual orientation. It's not really about us. It's a system that can't stand the idea that people can be free of the limitations of gender roles.

Championing the rights of transgender people will free gay, lesbian, and bisexual people. And transgender people will also benefit.

The Manly Response is War

September 11, 2001. An unspeakably horrific, devastating, sorrow-filled, emotionally draining day.

We saw thousands of Americans die, buildings crumble, and our own planes under the control of men who wanted to inflict unforgettable damage, take many lives, and make their statement at all costs. There can be no excuse for such hellish terrorism.

The "President of the United States" issued a brief statement and remained in silence and seclusion for most of the day. Others criticized him for this, but I was thankful. A man I did not trust was better silent. The prospect that he would eventually open his mouth with a response only added more fear to my day.

When he spoke, it was what I had feared. And national leaders from both political parties climbed all over themselves to line up behind him. Congress would unanimously give him a blank check to take all necessary force in response.

"This is not terrorism; this is war." We were now going to "rid the world of evil," he told us.

The rhetoric that our country uses to describe its approach to almost everything soon began to define our approach to the actions of 19 terrorists and their supporters. Our politicians continued "war" talk even before we knew who the "enemy" was. We just had to do something to someone for this. Someone, somewhere has to pay.

The word "retaliation" was everywhere. Our government leaders began to deny that this was just a "criminal act."

It didn't matter that these were dastardly criminal acts that require justice, proof, convincing a fairly "impartial" panel of jurors or a judge, protecting our rights, and political silence so as not to unduly influence. But to frame this as war instead, requires destruction of something and someone, public speeches and bravado, "collateral damage," scapegoats, and giving up our civil liberties.

Within a day our "president" called this "The First War of the 21st Century." What was left of the twin towers of the World Trade Center was "Ground Zero" as if it were the scene of a foreign atomic bomb. CNN, a network which seems to salivate for war and the ratings generated by its around-the-clock coverage, began using the banner "America's New War."

I listened to talk shows where many callers urged caution, spoke of fear of the escalation that results from "retaliation," the need for understanding, and even their disappointment in the rhetoric of our leaders. Yet the media ground on with "War" language. NBC, owned by General Electric, which has a large stake in producing military equipment, and the other networks joined the politicians. What was needed, they all knew, was what we had done before: to sell the American people on the idea that this is a "War." Repeat it long enough and often enough and it will be our vocabulary.

We were all quickly supposed to change our black mourning clothes to red, white, and blue, as if such "patriotism" would help us process the loss of human beings. We were to see this as an "Attack on America" itself and were told that the reason for this attack was that "these people hate our freedom and liberty."

Nothing was said about how we've trained most terrorist leaders or of the decades of self-serving, often anti-democratic, U.S. foreign policy that people around the world were supposed to stomach, and which had recently become more blatant with our pulling out of world conferences and established treaties and protocols. Of course, we never pulled out of conferences we dominated that involved American investments and trade.

We are a country that was born in war. We were the people the British called "terrorists," killing the British while hiding behind rocks and trees. And we've been calling our efforts "war" ever since, as if we can't fathom any other approach to life. Think beyond the Vietnam War to the war on poverty, the war on drugs, the war on crime, the war on illiteracy, the war on AIDS.

It's not that we've "won" a lot of these either. And the "wars" we have won have only produced temporary "victories." It sounds quite naive today to think that World War I was called "the war to end all wars," but it was. We humiliated Germany in the "victory" of that first world war and, of course, they've never bothered us since.

But "war" is our model. It's one of the conditioned responses of "real men" in the Unites States. Real men don't sit and talk. They don't take their time to consider history, to listen carefully to the opinions of others, and to see what part they may have played in all this.

Real men steel themselves, and strike back, unquestionably, decisively, quickly. Real men get angry. Real men see this as attacks on our honor and virility, our manhood. And they see that the retaliation must be even greater to "teach them a lesson" and restore our "pride," that is, our manhood. As one man said, "We need to throw everything we've got at them."

I am reminded of Malcolm X saying "Anger clouds intelligence." Or of Mahatma Gandhi's: "An eye for an eye and a tooth for a tooth, and the whole world is blind and toothless." Or of John Stoltenberg's "You can't love manhood and justice."

We've tried war for generations and now have begun what may become the second-bloodiest century in history, the last being the bloodiest so far. And we can't seem to give it up because, I believe, it is a part of conditioned, straight, manhood. It's installed in our men through fear and terror — fear of not being manly enough and being accused of being too soft, too effeminate, too queer. If this kind of manhood is in charge, then it defines our leadership and approach.

To go against it all is to be thought of as "un-American," as "not being a patriot." But that's what anyone is called who refuses to follow the dominant crowd. Feminists, anti-war protesters, suffragettes, civil rights activists, unionists, and gay liberation leaders, have all been put down as "un-American."

To say there is a way of greater, real, permanent healing, a way that doesn't interpret the actions of others as threats to our manly being, a way that will not feed the war machine and "the military-industrial complex" that President Eisenhower warned us against, may be called "un-American." But someone has to be courageous enough to stand up and break the cycle of escalation and violence.

Right now I can only imagine what could be achieved if the world's most powerful nation had the vision to lead us out of the cycles of violence instead of participating in them. But I think the most powerful nation is just too scared to do it.

Feeling Good about Feeling Bad

I did everything I could to be in the best position outside Gate 16 so that I would get as long a glimpse as possible of my sweetheart as he walked down the jetway to a plane that would take him to a city that seemed far away. For a while the great times that we have when we're together would take a backseat because I already missed him.

When he disappeared from sight, I looked through the window for a second at his plane, as if somehow I would see him again. I then turned and walked back to the car for the hour drive home — plenty of time to feel how much I missed him and to reflect on the experiences of being together both in the hard work of naming the personal issues we were committed to face together and in the overwhelming enjoyment of all that we experienced in our togetherness.

For a few moments I heard an old tape playing in my head about feeling this way: What's "wrong" with me that I feel so "bad"? But I knew that came from old messages, and soon caught myself in the warmth of the revelation that missing someone this deeply was a gift. I smiled as I thought about how wonderful it is to have someone to miss this much. This "bad" feeling was loving, caring, and human. It was actually good.

Society trains us to devalue certain feelings, to consider them "bad" in the hope of providing us with the stuff that will take them away. Not surprisingly, this is a money-making approach since the stuff to do so is usually sold to us, and often addictive.

Our culture also defines what feelings we're not supposed to have, or, at least, admit we have. Women are not to get angry or show anger, or not to feel too much self-confidence. And men are not supposed to feel afraid (except sometimes in culturally approved battles with each other, as long as they don't act on it) or hurt or confused, or at least not admit this without jeopardizing their real manhood.

And we're also taught how to react when we have these "bad" feelings. Men are conditioned to flip almost unconsciously into abstraction whenever hurt, fear, or confusion arise. They think in terms of principles not persons, about precedents and laws, not feelings. They move out of the details and ambiguities of relational life to hide in the maths and sciences of the analytic life, and in engineering the "solutions."

Or, men are conditioned to isolate from these feelings, either by flipping into that familiar secondary emotion, anger, or into addictions such as television, alcohol and sex. Sometimes they isolate right in front of others as any woman knows when she is sitting across from a man and senses that he's not really there.

"Are you listening?" she might ask; and he'll assure her: "Oh yes!" But then he'll often be caught having forgotten something she vividly remembers later. That there-but-not-there experience, results from something in the environment, or conversation triggering the emotions society says it's "bad" for men to have.

Or, men are conditioned to minimize these emotions as "women's stuff." In our culture, women are allowed the freedom to feel hurt, fear or confusion, but this is put down. How many homophobic men when seeing the buffed bodies of an *International Male* catalogue have concluded, to save their feelings about it, that, "they're all gay (not really male by gender conditioning) anyway."

Women who have these emotions are conditioned to believe their emotions have little value; certainly not as valuable as cold, hard, manly reasoning. They are conditioned to deny their emotions, or isolate from them in out-of-body experiences.

Or they are taught to transfer their emotions, especially when they involve anger, to more acceptable "women's" emotions: hurt and confusion, the one's men minimize. That's why Mahrya Monson's poem, "Anger," speaks volumes:

Women are denied the release of swearing,
The fist driven through the wall,
Reverberations echoing through the neighborhood.
Sometimes we are allowed to slam doors.

When we were children,
We were told,
    "Don't be angry."
    "It's not nice to be angry."
Is that why
ANGER
GIVES ME A STOMACHACHE
MAKES ME
SHAKE
CAUSES ME TO FEEL
SICK?
I have often shed tears in anger.
Is that a more acceptable way
                    for a
Woman
            to be
A*N*G*R*Y?

Feelings in themselves are no more than feelings meant to be felt. We can choose whether to act, base our thinking on, or make decisions on the basis of these feelings. Those emotions society tells us are "bad" and we shouldn't have, are important. They are often messages from our past, about what happened to us to install these feelings which something in the present has triggered.

But society is also suspicious of good feelings that arise spontaneously — of play ("That's childish; replace it with competition."), of love and romance ("You can't trust those either; they'll let you down."), of joy ("Postpone it.") and of our own lovability ("You're not; don't over-rate yourself; you don't deserve it.").

We can choose to deal with our emotions or not. None is "bad," none unmanly or unwomanly. They are part of our life.

Some are from the past and useless in the present. Others are from the present and really are based in what's happening in front of us. They warn us, confirm us, and enhance our todays. And we must sort them out to be who we really are.

And none of those feelings that tell us we are anything less than whole, complete, loving, and lovable are true, because the fact is we are no less than whole, complete, loving and lovable. That's true no matter how we feel.

Sisters Who Redefined Our Freedom

When rich, white males turned the Declaration of Independence's "All men are created equal" into the original U.S. Constitution, they took "men" quite literally. Their constitution made landed, white men equal. They denied the vote to everyone else. "Taxation without representation" ended — for them. Freedom in its fullest form was limited to them. When we immortalize these founding fathers we forget that they didn't include most of us in the American dream.

It took "radical" and "disruptive" people who were willing to give blood, sweat, and tears to change that constitutional discrimination so freedom would be something legal regardless of gender, race, or skin color. We white males, even if we are gay, hate to admit that we have historical privileges others haven't.

Change came about often because women, often people who today would identify as lesbians, forced that change upon us against the odds. There were courageous, subversive men too, but the Americans who most often identified the need for change were not privileged, white males.

A careful look at U.S. history reminds us of the place of our sisters, many our lesbian sisters, in the struggle for freedom. Nineteenth century women who formed domestic partnerships with other women were more likely to be pioneers for broadening liberty.

They often began as abolitionists. Their struggles would turn to women's suffrage as a result of their experiences advocating for the end of slavery. Extending the vote to men of color was only a step, not enough, but in this too they participated fully and led in both movements.

The most well-known sister was Susan B. Anthony, who began her public career as a lecturer for the American Anti-

Slavery Society. In 1869, after forming a close relationship with Elizabeth Cady Stanton, they both called the first post-Civil War women's suffrage convention which formed the National Woman Suffrage Association. The ultimate result was the extension of voting rights to women.

Seldom, however, are women such as Anthony recognized for their affection for other women. Our culture prefers to "straighten up" our heros and heroines.

Anthony's most well-known beloved was Emily Gross of Chicago, a married woman. As Anthony wrote in a letter to a niece, "I shall go to Chicago and visit my new lover — dear Mrs. [Emily] Gross — en route to Kansas . . . ." Such sentiments are found throughout these movements and are documented in Lillian Faderman's new book *To Believe in Women: What Lesbians Have Done for America — A History* (1999).

The facts are that we owe the extension of our freedoms to the work of our sisters, and our lesbian sisters. And we gay, white males do not know the greater strength it took for these women to overcome the layers of prejudice they faced.

We too have known discrimination, been threatened, hurt, killed, ridiculed, and rejected for being gay. We know what it takes to face that. But we have little idea of what it means for a woman who is also a lesbian to stand up against both the heterosexism and sexism of our culture, and often us, to lead movements for liberation.

We are good at denial of the depth of women's issues. We forget what it must have been like for girls to hear the same early taunts we heard as boys about how bad it was to be, look, or act "like a girl." We know little of what it meant to be told your value and being is so inferior that you need the approval of the gender you are not in order to be valuable.

We have no idea what it means not only to be told how inferior a woman is but to suspect you don't even fit this definition of an inferior gender because you love other women. We don't realize the depth of being told to "bite your tongue" and never let the anger out that bottles up inside our sisters.

And we won't know until we face our own male gender conditioning, recognize that even as gay men we have privileges
our lesbian sisters don't have, and face our own attitudes and
actions regarding women. We were not born this way. All of this
is how we were conditioned. But as long as we deny the nature
of our culture's conditioning around gender, we will not fully
benefit from what our sisters have done for us.

And the final thing they've done for us is called "feminism."
We men are not supposed to like "feminism." We are supposed
to put it down, criticize feminists as some evil, anti-male force.
That's what the system is teaching us.

But those who have argued for equal rights for women (a
definition of "feminism") have done us a favor, because, if we
are listening closely, we will see that they have led again in
extending freedom for all of us.

Their "radical" notions, criticized today by a frightened,
conservative backlash, have helped us see that homophobia
is a weapon of sexism, that limited gender definitions are used
against gay men as well as women. They have shown us that
the oppression of gay men has more to do with the issues feminism raised than anything else.

That's why if two heterosexual men walk down almost any
street in America and decide to hold hands, they'll be treated
like gay men too. It has nothing to do with who is having sex
with whom, and a lot to do with the fact that these men are not
acting the way "real men" should. The oppression of gay men
is a subset of sexism.

We owe our sisters for that insight as well. They are leaders
in the next extension of equality in the U.S. In response, the
least we can do is make sure we aren't a part of putting any of
our sisters down.

Listening to Our Sisters

In many gay communities I've visited, people have asked me how the rifts between women and men can be healed. Frustration exists on all sides when leadership issues erupt publicly in angry disagreements between gay men and lesbians. Often, just at those times when the community is about to make its greatest strides, battles break out in the open and divide us so that we lose our effectiveness.

Well, men, the underlying cause is sexism. And if we don't go into denial about it, don't find it challenging some need we have to do everything just right, or don't descend into our own victim position about how we too have been hurt by women, we can be a major part of the healing that our communities need.

Our task is to face our own, often unconscious and unintentional, sexism. And if we have been brought up in this culture, or the many others where men still control society's institutions, we cannot help but be sexist. We are like fish in water, and need to hear that the fact is that we are wet.

Now, men are not inherently sexist; we didn't ask for this conditioning, it was not a free choice, and we don't deserve it. And sexism hurts us, not just our sisters. Homophobia is its major weapon, and gay men are one of sexism's targets. While sexism lasts, we will be targeted.

The fact is, we can choose to change it. And for our own survival, not just for the health and welfare of our sisters, we need to start now.

Of course, we'll make mistakes. Personal and cultural healing is messy. If our sisters love and trust us, they will point those mistakes out. And we will correct our mistakes, not deny them.

There are many aspects to this:

• no more lesbian jokes told by us (yes, lesbians can tell them, just as we can call each other "fag" though the term is offensive when outsiders use it);

• no longer calling grown women by the diminutive "girls";

• no more criticisms of women who do not conform to the culture's definition of "feminine";

• no longer calling assertive women "bitches";

• recognizing that sexism made many of our mothers the primary caretakers who did their best to follow men's advice while being told by these male "experts" to ignore their own instincts.

However, the most important thing, the very beginning, and maybe the hardest, is for us to just listen carefully to our sisters.

Men in our culture are conditioned not merely to listen, but to "fix" women, solve their problems, know what they need, give unsolicited advice, and come up with clever responses. What we really need to do is none of these things.

We need to listen because women are fully capable of fixing themselves. At best we can be their supportive allies as they break from all the messages they received about their value, beauty, and issues being defined by men.

And that means we must listen, listen for our own healing as well as theirs, listen to their stories and the anger they have because the system has treated them as lesser beings.

When as boys we were criticized with: "You walk like a girl; You talk like a girl; You throw a ball like a girl; You have a name that sounds like a girls name; You carry your books like a girl; You run like a girl" — we learned that the worst thing we could be like was a girl. And they learned the worst thing to *be* was a girl. They are sick and tired of it, and we really are too.

Girls, they were also told, aren't supposed to get angry. But we all get angry, and the culture's sexism itself ought to make us angry. So, women need to express all the anger they weren't supposed to express. They need to get it out, so they can get to the deeper hurts that need healing.

And, they may express that anger at men, at us, because men have run the system and, on the whole, have benefitted from it. They may express it when we personally don't think we need it.

When a woman tells me, "That was sexist" and does so in anger — even if she were to tell me "I hate all you men" — I can go into my victim role with "but we men have been hurt too" (for most men have been hurt by a woman in their life — a mother, teacher, etc. — but that is not systemic sexism).

I can dismiss their anger and their personal histories by just writing them off as "man haters." I can further diminish their humanity by walking away to save my own feelings.

Or I can listen, listen carefully to what is really being said by this woman who stands before me. I can see that this woman is saying two seemingly contradictory things: "I hate what you did" (or even: "I hate you"), and, "I'm telling you this because I don't want to hate you, I don't want you to be anything less than the best you can be. I want to have a healthy relationship with you. I'm not sure I can trust you, for you may go back into your conditioned manhood stuff, but I'm going to give this a try. Will you stick with me in this?"

We cannot be full human beings if we aren't allies for each other. And, men, we need to learn how to be allies for those who have been the major victims of the sexism of our culture.

We have to give up our perfectionism, be willing to make mistakes, and love and be secure enough in ourselves to listen to the other half of the human species — the half that has been told just to look pretty, don't act smart, be quiet, follow the leadership of men, value men's ideas over your own, and transfer any feelings of anger you do have to tears or bodily aches.

Leaving out half the human race, was never how it was meant to be. We should all be angry about this, for it's not only our sisters' issue, but our own.

We'll learn a lot by listening to women. They have a lot to teach us, if we're willing. And, men, it's past time we did this.

Sex

The Minor Details

So, Where's the Sex in All of This?

I want to say this clearly. Sex, and I do mean genital activity and everything surrounding it, is really a great thing. It's a means of communicating between people that can embody a range of possible messages.

It can be intimate and close or detached and distant, whether it's sex with a committed partner or a "one night stand." If we are clear about what we're doing and why we're doing it, we can choose what any sexual encounter will mean and what it communicates.

But that's the rub, so to speak. We ourselves are seldom clear about what's going on when we have sex.

Our culture has done everything it can to pass on its sickness about sex to all of us. And it has installed its sick messages into us so deeply that we have difficulty sorting them out and clearing them from both our consciousness and our unconscious.

We are told that sex is the key to everything. Sex sells. And the insecurities that our society installs in us drive home the message that buying something else will make us more sexually appealing according to the standard of "appealing" that's driven by consumption.

Then, we're taught, such sexiness will get us the human closeness we really want. But that's a false promise. If it were true, we might actually find closeness and quit buying stuff. Our ravenous economy can't afford that level of fulfilment. So, even those who make this promise know it's a lie.

We're also conditioned to believe that sex is not just one of many possible ways of expressing closeness but a means to achieve closeness with someone. For men, the further message is that sex is the only means of getting close. This psychological pressure behind conditioned male sexuality is so insistent that sex takes center stage dysfunctionally, completely out of proportion to its reality.

And this need actually turns sex into a way of distancing. The fantasizing that substitutes for really being there with someone, is even encouraged by some psychologists so that sex becomes a means of staying away from people while it is hooked to some dream. And when two males get together, male conditioning in this matter is doubled, causing all sorts of difficulties in same-sex relationships, often including the inability to connect "hot sex" with love and commitment. Some psychologists counsel women to get with this kind of program too.

The dominant religious sexual morals ingrained in us successfully divert our attention in order to maintain the political, economic, and religiously controlling status quo. With all the condemning and shaming messages about sex, our psyches fill with guilt over our sexualities. This ensures that our energy will never threaten what's really wrong with this culture — the systemic, anti-human institutions that are profit-oriented and coping-oriented and not functional for human beings and their healing. It's our personal sicknesses that need changing, we've come to believe, not the crazy-making system.

When we actually act sexually with all these messages, we run up against the further cultural message that sex is somehow dirty and shameful, particularly if we happen to enjoy it. Isn't that old message something like: "Sex is dirty; save it for the one you love?"

President Bill and Aide Monica were the actors in the drama some have dubbed a "Monicathon." It played on this message of shame, with Congress and the media denying that it was "about sex" while they voyeuristically went into details about oral sex as if that were sordid itself.

If this general message of dirt weren't bad enough, LGBT people are taught that their sex is even dirtier. The shame that LGBT people carry is doubled.

Sometimes this means that we get high with the thrill of breaking the rules, of doing something "dirty," of possibly getting caught, or of being a rebel against all the limits of parents and authorities. That high has little to do with the person we're with and loses its appeal when it's not directed against our oppressors.

At other times our shame acts out in guilt: in the inability to look into the eyes of the real person we're in bed with, or the lack of desire to even speak to the person with whom we've just cum because the whole thing after the orgasm feels dirty and shameful. We just want to escape that shame as quickly as possible by falling asleep or bolting for the door.

LGBT national politics is dominated by this shame today. Michael Warner in his important book, *The Trouble with Normal: Sex, Politics, and the Ethics of Queer Life* (1999), exposes a "politics of shame" that lies behind much national LGBT leadership as it works to put homosexual sex out of sight in order to gain acceptance and love from the dominant "straight" culture (That's "straight," the culturally-conditioned role and its restrictions, not "heterosexual," the orientation.).

These leaders argue that we must look more like "straight people" outwardly to gain their love. But that strategy hasn't ended racism or any other oppression.

The deeper problem is that the people of a heterosexual orientation we want to impress are also sick about sex. They need the help of people who are outside the sickness in order to see this. They don't need us to join them in promoting the dysfunction. They don't need us to say, "I don't want to be known by my sexual orientation."

They don't need us to live out our shame so we reinforce their ideas about our shamefulness. They don't need us to talk about being "post-gay" as if we have attained anything other than what Urvashi Vaid called a "virtual equality" (rather than a real one) in her analysis of where we've come (*Virtual Equality,* 1995).

LGBT people have the possibility of getting beyond all this. They can be healthy models to counter the "normal" culture of sexual sickness. We really can. But not if we set our goal on looking like "normal people," and not if we don't get clear about what this fun, playful, intimate thing called sex really is.

δex That's Not δtraightjacketed

"**P**ublic arguments against homosexuality are influenced by negative attitudes toward sex that is only an act of intimacy and pleasure." That's what Pepper Schwartz and Virginia Rutter pointed out again at the end of the twentieth-century in their 1998 book, *The Gender of Sexuality.*

No matter how tired and out-dated the old arguments seem to us, we continue to hear objections to same-sex marriage based upon the idea that "marriage" is for procreation. Yet because any person or any couple can raise a child, there's got to be more to this complaint than whether or not LGBT people can raise children.

And there is more. Since those who are defining the debate define homosexuality exclusively and obsessively in terms of what "you people do in bed," not love, intimacy, commitment, and romance, what they really mean is that morally good sexual activity must potentially lead to procreation.

It doesn't seem to matter how we respond, or how often we point out the obvious — that not all heterosexual couples do or can have children. The right-wing, and many others who still think in their terms, desperately need to deny that same-sex genital activity can ever be life-giving or love-making.

To picture same-sex sexual activity as something other than incomplete, unhealthy, and unfulfilling, might begin to open people up to the idea that gay sex is indeed fully human and intimate, not debased at all. That means making LGBT relationships and sex unappealing has to be a constant goal.

The long history of religious support for the idea that the exclusive purpose of sexuality is baby-making, an idea now most often defended by the Vatican, still lingers as long as these arguments are raised against equal rights for LGBT people. The necessary potential of making a baby just remains a part of "straight" thinking about good sex. And denying birth

control to women ensures that they will experience less pleasure in sex.

Of course, the idea that good sex is exclusively for procreation isn't necessarily a part of natural, unconditioned heterosexual sex either. Heterosexuals think sex is fun and pleasurable too. They want more of it and want it more fulfilling.

It's just that society conditions them to act and think
"straight." So, in spite of how much heterosexual people don't
live up to the ideal of "straight" sex, they too are supposed to
feel guilty and ashamed if they are having just plain fun sex.

Straight women are expected to feel less than the ideal if
they can't birth their own child. And straight men and women
are supposed to feel that good sex takes place only in a marriage that can bring children into being even if they aren't having fun with their partner in the process.

Few straight men are brought up to allow themselves to talk
with their partners about what gives them pleasure in sexual
activity. It's just not "manly." Few women feel they can talk to
their husbands without it cracking a fragile masculine ego.

So, they're left to fantasize about pleasurable sexual activity. Some seek their fantasies in greener pastures elsewhere,
hoping that what they're looking for in sex will just happen so
they won't have to talk about it with someone else either. They
may even feel guilty, ashamed, and angry about having the
desire for pleasurable sex and for failing to fulfil their desire.

For anyone to believe that the purpose of sex is giving and
receiving pleasure is to break free of this straightjacket. That's
why the out and open existence of LGBT people disrupts the
straight pattern. LGBT people are understood to embody
sex for no other reason than pleasure. This does, as the Gay
Liberation Front pointed out decades ago, disrupt the dysfunction of a culture that is deeply sexually ill.

Of course, there are many reasons to have sex. To create
another life is one. To express closeness with or commitment
to another human being we love is another. But whatever else
it is, sex is also fun, pleasurable, playful, and free.

Yet in the midst of a culture that basically uses sex to generate consumers, discussing the pleasure of sex out loud is not a "straight" thing to do. If you think it is, just start your next conversation with your friends with: "I really like sex." Watch how they react and where that conversation goes.

So, how can we break out of this cultural sickness? How can we say that sex is fun, and good, and an important element of our closest relationships, something we cherish with those we cherish? Since we are already out as people who have sex for pleasure, since we already claim no longer to be "straight," it ought to be easy.

The problem is that we too internalize the messages of the straight culture around us about what morally good sex is. And by the lingering dominant definition, we can never have it.

We know that the culture around us still hates to think about us having good sex. And we live in the shame of that, trying to cover our own nakedness with what looks like little more than the fig leaves that Eve and Adam and Steve wore in that ancient garden.

We don't want straight people to think we find pleasure in sex even if it's with a committed partner. Through our own acts of shame, we politically play it down as much as possible.

By doing that we communicate to the broader culture that we are ashamed of being sexual beings: "I just happen to be gay." "I'm just like you." "Look, we're not just defined by what we do in our bedrooms." Or, to take a phrase from the Christian Gospels and make it negative: "We don't want to be known by the people we love." And the dominant culture smiles back at our shame.

Instead of being pioneers in cultural healing around sex, we buy into, support, and collude with the cultural sickness. So, like the dominant culture, our sexual acts become more of an obsession, a forbidden desire, and less an intimate, human activity that has an important place in the scheme of things.

It's our decision. Do we really want our sex to be "straight-acting"? Do we really think the sexual model of our dominant culture is healthy? Or do we want to live on our terms for us with those we love? ...And celebrate pleasure in the process.

Priests, Sexual Abuse, and Sexual Addiction

The Roman Catholic Church has done nothing less than any large, multi-national business organization would have done in reaction to a scandal. This, of course, bothers people who expect more from religious institutions than other international bureaucracies such as Enron, Tyco, WorldCom, and Global Crossing. Still, there are others who assert that the Church really should be run like a business.

As priests were accused of sexual abuse and pedophilia, the Church's immediate and routine response was cover-up and denial. The larger the organization, the farther away its top-level executives can "transfer" managers from their crimes. There are also more branch office opportunities for hiding employees.

What challenged this self-protecting pattern to some extent was what often brings meaningful, radical change in a society — the persistent objections of common folk. They were tired of being a part of the cover-up because the price they were paying for protecting the institution was their own emotional healing. To quote Fannie Lou Hammer, they were "sick and tired of being sick and tired."

To protect its reputation, the organization next tried to settle with the victims. It didn't want questions raised about whether something systemic was going on, whether its very structure, values, processes, and leadership were really at fault.

Then it argued that the abusers were isolated cases. They were just "bad apples" that haven't spoiled the barrel itself. It's the same way the Los Angeles police department has used the "bad apple" argument through one scandal after another and another and another.

Finally, under continuing pressure from those who were trying to end what was hurting them, the Church moved into a "damage control" mode. It agreed to turn over "necessary" information to law enforcement authorities. Who knows how many cases it won't turn over because people haven't threatened to sue?

That's the story as reported, but what's missing from these news reports?

First, what about the complaints of priestly abuse from women? About 50% of the almost 4,000 members of SNAP (The Survivors Network of those Abused by Priests) are women.

Society takes the story with more seriousness when men are the victims of sexual activity. Women are treated as less important in such matters, as if their victimhood is to be expected. Real men aren't supposed to be victims of sexual activity. They should be in charge.

Second, concentrating on the abuse of boys plays into homophobic prejudices that connect pedophilia with homosexuality. Why are we surprised when we hear Church leaders acting as if the way to "solve" the problem is to psychologically screen out bad priests and meaning those with a homosexual orientation?

Third, the fact that the sexual abuse that has come to light is associated with the Roman Catholic Church, plays into the lingering, often hidden, anti-Catholic sentiments of right-wing Protestants. Their deeply-held, long-standing prejudices often surprise people, especially Catholics. The most conservative Protestants are the ones who still put down Roman Catholicism as a "cult," yet use it for their own purposes (as allies against evolution, women's choice, women's full equality, and homosexuality) when they find it politically advantageous.

The existence of sexual abuse by the clergy beyond the Catholic Church is another societal secret. Though it apparently occurs in similar proportions, it's widely swept under the rug by denominations and local churches. And these cover-ups are successful unless media or police get involved who are willing to break the history of colluding with Christianity and its powerful institutions.

But what's missing most from this story is what it says about dominant attitudes toward sexuality in our culture. Sex is useful economically and morally. Sex sells our products and life-styles. And sex is a favorite device to shame and demean the sexually active. Sex is also useful for putting down minorities (racial, sexual, and otherwise) who are pictured as more sexually active, even dangerously so, than the "normal," "civilized," and "mature" among us.

As an expert on addictions, Anne Wilson Schaef has much to say about all this as a part of our societal illness. In her *Escape from Intimacy: Untangling the 'Love' Addictions: Sex, Romance, Relationships* (1989), she writes that sexual addiction is "of epidemic proportions in this society and is integrated into the addictiveness of society as a whole." It is, in fact, one of the addictions most woven into our society as "normal."

This is obvious when we listen to Schaef's definition of sexual addiction – "an obsession and preoccupation with sex, in which everything is defined sexually or by its sexuality and all perceptions and relationships are sexualized." There is little question that this defines mainstream U.S. society, including the training of LGBT people.

Now, we are used to thinking of sexual addiction as an out-of-control search for sexual action. In that sense, pedophilia and other sexual abuse are often ways of acting out of a sexual addiction.

But what some may not want to face, Schaef explains, is celibacy as sexual addiction. When celibacy is a struggle, it's a sign that one is acting out of an addiction, a preoccupation and obsession with sex. And when any institution focuses on sexuality and struggles with it, that's a sign that the institution itself is promoting, even built upon, sexual addiction.

Though we've been taught to respond that celibacy is a struggle for everyone, it's actually not when it arises out of a healthy inner process that leads a person to a place where they are naturally celibate. But denial, remember, is also a mark of an addict, and the struggle with sexuality, which our dominant institutions might say is normal, is denial and not natural. It's the mark of an obsession that may even take the form of repulsion.

Patrick Carnes (*Out of the Shadows: Understanding Sexual Addiction*, 3rd. ed. 2001) identifies a repressive sexual addiction to include persons who are obsessed with repressing sexuality, their own and other's. This includes, specifically, sexual righteousness, obsession with sexual purity, nonintegrated celibacy, and religious sexual obsession.

Addictions function to keep us from dealing with the issues that could change our lives. And the obsession with and repression of sex and sexuality by the institutions of our culture functions to keep society and its institutions unchanged, no matter how unhealthy the institutions are.

As people who grew up in this society, we LGBT people have also been conditioned to assume the truth of this dominant, addictive process. However, it's now our choice whether we continue to buy into the values and justifications of the process that keeps the sexual addictions going or we choose to live alternative, healthy lifestyles that are not those a sexually sick society has set before us.

Romance

The Minor Details

A Valentine's Day Romance Beyond the Myth

I'm one of those who believe romance is both important and fun. It's a true test of vulnerability as well as the ability of love to be playful. To let go, express how one really feels about another, and expect that other to honor those feelings and be vulnerable in return, is a commitment of sometimes frightening proportions.

I believe that romance doesn't have to end. It deepens as long as people grow. I believe that deepening requires real personal growth. It means I have to work on my own issues first, not on "our" issues.

There's actually nothing like a deepening relationship to unpack our past baggage and spread it all over the living space. We may find we're walking on a mine field of old issues that we didn't know existed or thought were sufficiently buried so they wouldn't bother us again.

We may even vow that this time we won't make past mistakes — but that thinking means we're using this relationship to fix past relationships. That's not living with the people we love in the present.

To help us cope, there's Valentine's Day — not surprisingly in our capitalist culture a chance to profit from romance. Cards, flowers, chocolates, and parties with our favorite addictions, are a part of its economics. It's big business.

February fourteenth celebrates our culture's mythology of romance, a mythology that builds unrealistic expectations, focuses on fleeting feelings of closeness, and becomes a hiding place from ourselves and the world. Psychologists have pointed out that romance can be an addiction, a way not to feel what it is necessary to feel in order to really be present with another.

Our basic romantic myth is that if we are really lucky, that one person will find us who will fulfil our needs, maybe all of them. And this one human being will become the sole object of our love, intimacy, and deepest secrets.

Women are told that the right man will do this: "I was half, but now I'm whole." For the mainstream this means women are trained to go around acting like half a person — a very difficult job — to get that man. Men are told they can only get intimacy, caring, and honesty from the right woman, and that their intimacy needs will be met particularly in their bedroom.

To the extent that LGBT people participate in this myth, they not only act out the dysfunctions of the culture at large, but find it difficult to trust a same-sex partner. If I make myself vulnerable, I might get hurt. The myth really functions to keep us from authentic closeness.

But the myth also functions culturally as a drug that numbs us to what is happening around us. The preponderance of popular songs about romance, broken hearts, emotional helplessness, and dysfunctional relationships, isn't new. But today we seem to hear fewer songs about the workplace, social causes and movements, creating community, and people struggling together to overcome oppressions. The proliferation of oldie and classic rock radio stations makes sure that baby boomers can slip back to a mythically romantic past that will rescue their emotions from the present.

Focusing on this mythic romance is the surest way to keep us from seeking societal changes that will end what's really hurting us all in order to produce profits. It is directly related to another diversion: the emphasis on personal "ethics" which thinks in terms of individual right and wrong (that's your sex life) while ignoring the defects in societal ethics where the vulnerable starve, are abused, are ridiculed, and, when they react to it, are warehoused in "correctional" facilities.

While the institutions of religion early on defined "sodomy" in terms of this personal, diversionary ethic, they did so even in the face of the biblical texts themselves. The Hebrew prophet Ezekiel defined "sodomy" in social terms: "Now this was the sin of your sister Sodom: She and her daughter were arrogant, overfed and unconcerned, they did not help the poor and needy." (Few "literalists" ever took all of the Bible literally, especially when it called for radical social change in their lives that has economic consequences!)

What might romance be if we didn't limit ourselves to the myth? What might it be if romance became a choice, a conscious way of choosing to express the closeness we already have with another, not a desperate way to feel or get closer?

What if it rose out of the fact that people were learning how to be vulnerable, to share their hearts, emotions, and minds — to bare their souls because they demanded that their relationships be healing and healthy?

What if flowers arrived because you listen to me again and again as I reveal my fears about my life and our deepening and sometimes scary relationship?

What if a card came because you challenge me again and again to face my issues through fearless questioning born of the ruthless goal to make both your and my lives open to the universe?

What if I didn't rely on you to solve all my closeness needs, but freely chose you as the person with whom I want to struggle in both my and your growth?

What if I chose to be romantic with you because you have already set out on your heart's healing journey and I have too, and we have decided it's a journey we can take together?

What if a paper heart arrived in the mail because we had vowed to live totally in the present, not out of past messages and buried hurts from old "loves" and the adults of our childhoods — and we vowed to sort them out?

What if I sent chocolates because I've chosen to be there both with you and for you?

Beyond the mythology, romance is really a choice, and so is closeness. We can consciously choose both. And it can still make our hearts pound faster, bring a lump to the throat, and warm the soul on any cold February day.

That Romantic Touch

We met George and Jack in the "Nu-Towne Saloon" in Phoenix. It was one of those Sunday afternoon BBQ and cheap beer events that are common ways for gay bars to bring people in on the day before the work week begins.

George was 78 years old and Jack was 69. They had been together for 39 years. And they regularly went out together on Sunday to the Saloon.

They were probably the oldest people in the crowd. They knew that. They wondered if they were somehow out of place. After all, gay couples don't go out to bars after they've coupled up.

Instead I've heard couples criticize those who do. Maybe that's out of their own guilt about what bars meant to them when they were uncommitted singles. Maybe it's their fear that they couldn't just go out and have a good time together without replaying those unforgiven activities.

Such unexamined guilt (reflected in the claims in gay ads, "not into bar scene") keeps all of us from seeing such long-term relationships where we probably need to see them most. So, it was good they were there to break out of the gay pattern of huddling away together in couples to feel safe from the world.

They sat close together and most of the time they touched each other. Often I noticed George's hand just resting on Jack's thigh. Their touch was noticeable, tender, and romantic.

This was a date they kept together but not to leave the "gay scene" as some in the bar had apparently done through over-indulgence in the cheap beer. They were in that scene as two men who were still companions and partners and, as George told me, "still in love."

Valentine's Day can be a chance to ask what we've done to be romantic in the relationships that mean the most to us.

Have we bought the idea that "romance never lasts"? Have we listened to the patterns observers tell us couples go through in which romance is supposed to fade into something "deeper"? Or do we believe that romance is a choice in all of the small and larger things we do for our beloved.

Relationships do change, of course. One hopes they grow in positive ways.

They can become increasingly emotionally intimate, by pursuing personal and coupled growth, by sharing more and more of who we are, by taking more and more chances with the vulnerable places in our life, by valuing the good and being open to what needs work, by supporting each other's growth and pursuing what keeps us from being present in the relationship, by seeing all relationships as processes and never as finished products.

Cultivating romance is a part of the growth that we are freed to pursue, if we are growing as a couple.

Romance is words as well as actions. It's paying attention. It's treasuring the one who is before us. It's believing and assuming the best until the other has confessed they really meant less than the best.

It's saying "I love you" over and over again because you do. It's saying "I love you, too" in response because that's true.

It's admitting when it's hard to let love in because doing so has seemed to fail us in the past. It's looking in each other's eyes deeply and, as one looks, remembering why this person is special.

It's the unexpected deeds, large or small. It's the routine activities that come to have meaning like sacred rituals you can count on when you need to count on something — opening a car door, asking if there is anything I can do to help, keeping quiet company, preparing a meal together in the kitchen.

And it's touch. Touch is important in any relationship.

We know that without touch new born babies will die. But something happened as we "grew up" and were told we were "too big" for it.

Somewhere along the line we were touched inappropriately or violently. Somewhere along the way we were told we shouldn't need it or want it. Somewhere in our interactions we became afraid to ask for the touch we want or afraid of being rebuffed when we initiated the touch we gave. We were put out of touch with our physical and emotional humanness.

On top of that, homophobia taught us that we should be more separate, distanced, particularly in America. And it did one of the cruelest things of all to LGBT people.

It taught us that we shouldn't touch. It forbid us to touch publicly. And it made us feel that our touch is less than human, more like animals and deviants.

In spite of the old messages, the romantic touch, often casual and unconscious, is an important element to cultivate. Its absence is an important thing to notice. One's personal lack of interest in, or fears around, the romantic touch is an important response to investigate. And the belief that romance does not have to end is worth pursuing.

Say it again. Romance is a choice and also taking a chance. But don't wait for the world to approve, or your beloved to initiate, it again. Talk about it with your beloved before this Valentine's Day passes. Explain what you want and negotiate what you have. In fact, merely to begin the adventure of talking about the touch you want in your relationship sounds romantic.

What Do We Really Want from Cupid?

As the "seasonal" shelves clear of Christmas merchandise, stores refill them with potential sales for the next sale-ebration, the mid-winter holiday called Valentine's Day. The retail economy benefits by selling stuff that's supposed to prove that people really "love" one other.

If we're really "with it," we'll buy. It's just expected that we'll all go along with the definitions of "love" that a ravenous economy needs to further inflate corporate earnings.

Failure to recognize this day of national consumption can bring the coldness of a northern winter into the emotional depths of a relationship. And those of us who are well-conditioned by our culture and who don't receive these proofs of love, are supposed to feel left out, rejected, unfulfilled, and even somehow betrayed.

Such expectations are reminders of how many of us live as if what will save us from all our negative feelings is a boyfriend or girlfriend.

"I just want a relationship so badly," a twenty-two year old man told me. He had ended one less than a month earlier.

So, I suggested that he first learn to live as a single again or cultivate close friendships. (Yes, I said it to him in spite of the fact that I know that most such advice is usually unheeded.)

He was soon in another relationship, which took care of him for a few months. He just didn't want to face all the emotions that "being alone" brought up.

Relationships that function *so that* a person doesn't have to deal with herself or himself are "addictive relationships." Like any addictions, being in a relationship, any kind of romantic relationship as our culture defines them, keeps people from feeling emotions they just don't want to feel, examine, process, and leave — loneliness, abandonment, worthlessness, unworthiness, and hopelessness.

But that's not what romantic relationships, or even friendships, are meant to be. And down deep we know this, even if our dominant, consumerist culture thrives on romance addictions, just as it does on every other addiction.

If we try to be healthy, then, what do we really want in a romantic relationship?

We want someone who will keep walking beside us as we walk on our life path and who will encourage us to grow. We want someone who will nurture our growth, not inhibit it for their own frozen childhood needs.

We want to be able to be who we are and be accepted for that. We want someone who will not jump to negative conclusions but assume the best of us.

Down deep we even want that person to recognize when we have faltered, not act like we haven't because they can't handle our mistakes. We also want them to still believe we can do better. We want them to believe in us.

We want to be free to face our fears about relationships, — about being left, about being treated as less than human, about not deserving to be loved, about not deserving things to be as good as they can be, about not deserving to be with someone who is really good to us.

We want someone who will value our love for them, too, someone who has done their own internal work so they can accept our love. We want someone who knows that we are not those other people who have hurt them and that we cannot fix their past relationships, nor they ours.

We want them to share themselves and their deepest intimacies, to recognize their past hurts and to grow in their own healing around these hurts, not deny them or act them out on us. We want them to know what their own issues are, not project them on us.

We want them to include us in their life and also to have a life and path of their own that distinguishes them from us. We want to be able to encourage their personal and career growth and to be included in their life as much as we want them included in our life.

We want to share moments of deep, heart-moving emotions that arise out of the intimacies we share. We want to be reminded that passion is a lifestyle that feels deeply and honors the positive feelings we have for ourselves, our partner, our friends, and all life

We want our sexuality to be something we move in and out of in our relationship, not something that starts and stops abruptly and definitively. We want sex to be an expression of emotional and deep intimacy, not something we do desperately to feel intimacy or feel lovable. And we want sex to be fun and vulnerable.

All of this requires us to prepare ourselves for a relationship, even though most of us don't want to do that, or think we don't need it. But if we skip that part of our own journey, we'll never have what we really want. We'll settle for less, live through a "honeymoon" period, and then learn to cope, get along, and settle with unwritten and unspoken contracts with each other.

This means we have to face and feel the emotions that a relationship would otherwise keep us from feeling and healing. Just like heterosexual people (The straight world is no model for non-addictive relationships.), we will have to take the time and do the personal work it takes to deal with the feelings from which a relationship can never save us. That may include support groups, deliberate listening partnerships with friends, reading, reflection, and therapy.

He didn't know it, but I overheard my boyfriend summarize for a friend an idea that had made sense to him from the book by Kenneth D. George, *Mr. Right is Out There* (2000). "If we're going to find someone we really want, we first have to work on ourselves so that we're in touch with who we are. Then, who we really are, not some image we want to portray to the world, will attract people who are for us, not an image of us."

He's right. And the good news is: Yes, we can realize these better dreams. The fact is, though, it's up to us, not the planets, the stars, the moon, the sun, or even Cupid.

Those "Sweet Nothings"
Are Really Something

A 10-year, government sponsored study from the University of Washington, Seattle, concludes that how people are talking to each other at the first six months into a committed relationship predicts the success of the relationship with 87% accuracy.

It's not whether they communicate in the right words, whether they always agree on issues, whether they have the same interests, whether they like the same movies, music, or leisure time activities, whether they know how to "fight fair," whether they have great sex, or whether they come from similar backgrounds.

It's not what they actually say to each other. It's how they say it.

I'll bet that these other factors are still important and contribute to a relationship going more smoothly, but it's interesting that what predicted the long-term success of relationships was what the researchers called the "sweet nothings" that were part of a couple's every-day interactions. So, maybe on Valentine's Day, the results of this study call for a little reflection.

The study's co-author Sybil Carrere gave some examples: "if they expressed fondness and admiration for their partner, if they talked about themselves as a unit, if they finished each other's sentences, referenced each other when they told a story, and whether what came to mind was pleasant."

Of course, there's something deeper here that small expressions of affection like these reflect. It's something that requires a bit of emotional maturity on the part of the individuals who make up the couple. And it's the individuals who make up the couple – not the couple – who need a level of psychological health.

Sweet nothings represent a general approach to one's partner that involves an individual's inner security and willingness to show her or his feelings. It includes the ability to be vulnerable as well as playful. It's able to let go of game-playing, self-protective masks and drama, and the many forms of posturing that end up in stagnant relationship patterns that stifle the growth of both partners.

The approach evidences a measure of personal psychological health that assumes the best of one's partner and doesn't expect them to treat them badly. It may even, at times, be accused of seeing the partner through rose-colored glasses.

According to the study, the key predictors of a relationship not lasting for the long term were one partner's unwillingness to be influenced by the other (usually the man by the woman) and a partner starting quarrels "harshly" and with hostility. These, on the other hand, evidence the inability to become vulnerable, imperfect, and open with a partner.

Now, the study was done with married heterosexual partners. So, it doesn't take into consideration all the additional conditions LGBT people face.

All the institutions of our society at least pay lip service to the idea of long-term straight marriage. Few support long-term non-heterosexual relationships. And many LGBT institutions don't support them either. In spite of this, the somewhat surprising thing is how poorly most heterosexual marriages turn out – some ending in divorce and others just settling for a truce or a semi-comfortable co-existence.

But that's not surprising, given our culture's conditioning on how to be straight. Straight has rigid roles for "real" men and "real" women and how they are supposed to relate to each other – that is, in ways that are meant more to keep our economy going strong than to connect human beings in their full humanity.

So, LGBT people have had to create their own support systems if they wanted a long-term relationship. They have had to fight along with heterosexual allies to demand that institutions recognize that non-heterosexual relationships are not just sexual but also romantic and loving in the fullest sense of both terms.

And we still have more to confront than heterosexual couples. We have to dismantle the internalized homophobia that from our earliest years conditioned us to evaluate same-sex partnerships as less valuable, healthy, possible, trustworthy, and hopeful even before we knew we'd be in any.

We have to face the fact that internalized homophobia as the fear of closeness with the same sex has conditioned us to be more like competitors with our partners than whole-hearted vulnerable, relaxed, and playful lovers. If we persist in denying that this has affected us, we'll keep wondering what's happening in our relationships.

Now, in addition, we have to face the fact that our culture doesn't want us to express "sweet nothings" to each other. It wants even the idea to remain out of sight so that there's no possibility that people might see that we are loving, romantic, and capable of committed partnerships. Seeing our "sweet nothings" will contradict everything the heterosexist, homo-pitying, right-wing claims we are.

And even some of us think it's inappropriate to display in the littlest ways the affection we have for each other. We seem worried that "they" will only think of us as sexual.

So, what may be one of the most important elements in maintaining our relationships is exactly what society would deny us. And our fear of making ourselves vulnerable to our same-sex partner, or fear of what straight society may think, may do the same.

But it doesn't have to do it. We don't have to be the ones protecting society from us. We can choose to forget what others think and be the first same-sex couple people see expressing "sweet nothings."

We'd actually being doing them a favor. They can go back home and tell everyone what they've seen. They'll be the life of their parties. And the next time they see it, it won't be the first time for them. They can consider themselves more "with it."

Who would have thought that "sweet nothings" were not only good for our relationships but so powerfully subversive too?

So, if we're ready to make our relationships work, we can't deny ourselves and those we love the little expressions that make not only our relationships but our lives work. At the very least, then, we're going to have to make ourselves vulnerable to our partners. Unless, of course, we don't want our lives to work after all.

Seven Messages That Wreck a Relationship

A dmit it. LGBT relationships could be better.

But the messages about ideal relationships that we get from society actually keep us from having relationships that are all we'd like them to be.

No matter how damaging these messages may be, society isn't going to change them soon even though some people try to ignore them. There are too many economic benefits for the business world. Maintaining these sick messages sells products.

And when LGBT people join the parade and fit in, they do look "straighter." They look just like the ideal couple our culture is selling us. Yet they may also wonder why something still seems to be missing in relationships we think should be more than they turn out to be.

Here are seven false, unhelpful, but popular, messages keeping us stuck.

1) Being homosexual or bisexual hinders close, long-term relationships.

This idea is so universal and persistent, both blatantly and subtly, that we pick it up unconsciously. We blame lesbians and gay men for something, as if it's about all of them as a group, as if the fault is a characteristic of gay men or lesbians or bisexual people that's as inborn as sexual orientation: "All gay men are interested in is…." "Lesbians are always…." It's in our jokes, bitterness, and complaints about each other.

But the reality is, there's nothing "wrong" with anyone that has anything to do with their sexual orientation, no matter what the larger culture claims.

2) Same-sex closeness is naturally scary, uneasy, and insecure.

The dominant meaning of society's homophobia is "be too afraid to get close to your own sex." The purpose of this message is to turn boys into warriors, and girls into a warrior support system that keeps the warriors in charge and happy.

The installation of this fear creates suspect, self-destroying, competitive, and distancing same-sex relationships for people of all orientations. Even people who have accepted that they are not heterosexual, internalize homophobia.

An undercurrent of our closest relationships, as a result, is the fear that if we become vulnerable to the gender to whom we are attracted, we'll get hurt again, taken advantage of, made fools of, and, ultimately, abandoned. Same-sex relationships are not inherently scary. Society teaches us to fear same-sex closeness.

3) Out there is that one person who will take away my loneliness and feelings of incompleteness, and prove I am worthy of a relationship.

Though any good counselor will tell us this message is psychologically quite sick, it's still as common as dirt. People of every orientation are supposed to live as if they are half a person until someone makes them whole.

A good dose of therapy is the antidote, or a group of supportive, non-judgmental, empathetic, listening friends. The search to remove the feeling that something is missing in our lives by getting into a relationship puts a burden that's too heavy on a relationship. It can lead to settling, being lonely even in a relationship, or assuming that it's the "greener grass" of the next relationship that will be the answer.

4) Only the really lucky meet the right person.

If the stars are right and the moon's just right, if I'm in the right place and it's the right time, if my face looks right, if my hair's just right, if my body's just right, if I dress just right, if I smile just right, if I smell just right, if I'm the right age, if I drive the right car, if I say the right things, if I don't over-do it but I don't under-do it, then maybe, just maybe, I'll find the one Ms. or Mr. Right.

This romantic myth sells products by claiming they'll make us just right. It also makes me a victim of all these "ifs" instead of believing I'm all right and communicating to the world that I'm at ease with myself. If my relationship isn't fulfilling and promoting my growth, it's not about luck, but about my own choices.

5) This relationship is my chance not to make the same mistakes I made in the last one.

On the surface, this sounds reasonable. After all, we'd like to believe we're learning from our past mistakes.

But the way not to make the same mistakes in a new relationship is to clear up our old relationships and our problems related to them before we seek a new relationship. Otherwise we're trying to fix the old relationship in the middle of the new one. The new one becomes an active therapy session with a partner who's unaware that she or he is functioning as a counselor.

Growing beyond old relationships requires examining why we got into them, what needs they fulfilled for us that are not healthy but kept us in them, how we may have expected our partner to do what our parents didn't do for us, why we felt insecure, how we gave up our own growth and goals to be in the relationship, why we settled for less than everything, and probably more.

6) My love will change my partner to be what I want in her or him.

This common idea is a definition of codependency. It also keeps abused partners with their abusers. If I just love them more or enough, if I just change my actions for them, if I just try to understand them more, then everything will be okay.

Frankly, this doesn't work. And to love someone in order to get them to love me in return isn't love at all. It's unhealthy, a statement of our own feelings of unworthiness, of our need to get the love from our partner we didn't get from parents, and of our fear that the alternative to this relationship is being left alone. It's a clue that we need help, counseling, support.

7) Straight relationships provide the model for gay ones.

It looks inviting to settle down with all the "advantages" of dating and marriage straight people have. But it only takes a moment to remember that half of those marriages end in divorce and the other half aren't doing that well. Keeping up appearances, settling for unhappiness, accepting unspoken agreements to get by, and keeping too busy to face each other as vulnerable, intimate partners is rampant in straight relationships.

The key to better relationships isn't found in these messages. It's in rejecting them.

Becoming healthy individuals has to be our first goal. And when we no longer need salvation in that one right relationship, we'll be ready for the better relationships that we can develop, grow with, and work at to make them healthy affirmations of real life.

Being Families

The Minor Details

What Will Marriage Do for Us?

The debate in Vermont over the possibility of legal, same-sex marriage has raised quite a bit of excitement in LGBT communities around the country. Should this round prove as disappointing as Hawaii, it still won't have been fruitless. Each case slowly changes the nature of the issue so that it's never the same again.

In the meantime, two questions we need to consider are what we expect marriage to do for us, and what we will do for this "traditional" institution called marriage.

Conservative gay writer Andrew Sullivan has argued for gay marriage by claiming that "marriage civilizes men." Without it they are promiscuous and dangerous to society, I suppose. And single men, he must believe, are incapable of "civilizing" themselves.

Others argue that marriage will benefit LGBT people because it promotes stability, support, and legitimacy for our relationships. It will, they claim, not only make us better people in some way, but will make us look more legitimate to outsiders.

We are supposed to view marriage, then, as a solution to the problems in our relationships and a means to more acceptance by "straight" society.

Please.... Have these people looked at what "marriage" has done for "straight" society and heterosexual relationships?

It's quite clear that through the ages marriage has been an institution meant to order societies. It helps governments identify whose spouse belongs to whom, and whose children are the property of which adults. It helps structure matters of inheritance and legal responsibility. It has functioned to make legal and economic matters clear, usually at the expense of women and children.

Marriages were seldom arranged because two people were in love. They were arrangements between families, and the best marriages were the most advantageous for the families. One's romantic and sexual life, particularly for men, took place more often outside marriage, and this was acceptable as long as his marriage was acceptable.

So, how is this traditional institution that will save LGBT people (and civilize Andrew Sullivan) really fairing today?

Currently the divorce rate is about 50%. That doesn't mean that the other 50% are "successful" or even that the married are committed to each other in many ways. It merely means they have not divorced. Pretense, lack of deep communication, disappointments, infidelities, cheating, emotional distancing, unwritten contracts, and giving up on each other and on improving the relationship, are legion and obvious.

And this is the case with marriage *in spite of the fact* that most of the institutions in our society, from religion to government, support committed heterosexual relationships. Amazingly, with all of this support, the institution is still so frail, and it so often falls apart.

The issue is not that marriage is a heterosexual institution and that adding homosexual people to it will make a difference. The problem is that it is a "straight" one.

Marriage is in trouble because it is an institution that is defined by, and reinforces, a conditioned "straight" role on heterosexual people. Its standards are therefore too low. Its expectations are too inhuman. Its style is too consumer-driven. Its patterns and roles are too rigid. Its rewards are too superficial. And, no matter how much work the "straight" world is putting into this institution, there seem to be few who find satisfaction of their deepest human needs there.

Instead many blame its "failure" on us. It's silly but incredibly sad for our culture that "Defense of Marriage Acts" are essentially attempts to blame the failures of straight people and their marriages on LGBT people.

So, when we too can legally get married, what can this failing institution do for us? How will it make us any better?

It's unlikely that it will make us more "legitimate" in the eyes of straight people who are already blaming us for their own inability to make their own marriages something incredibly healing for them. It will not end homophobia or heterosexism.

In fact, it will probably actually promote both. As we strive to look like "straight" gays in these marriages, hiding our sexuality as if we're "nice gays" who don't do those things, it will legitimize a new kind of closet. We'll continue to turn on each other with the "good" gays blaming the "bad" gays for our problems.

Remember, the fact that marriages of people of color are legal in this country has done nothing to end racism. In fact, "acting white" makes little difference in white attitudes toward people of color. Whether people of color strive to copy "white" institutions or decide to affirm their own ethnic identities, they are criticized for "acting" or "flaunting." "The ideal American family" is a predominantly white picture. We've been good at blaming African-American families for problems in their communities.

There is no question that, legally, marriage will provide for same-sex couples the same legal benefits as heterosexual couples. We have the equal right to the same failed institutions as anyone else.

But, marriage as it is now defined will do little for the health and liberation of LGBT people.

Unless, we can do something for marriage.

The good news is we can. We can improve marriage to the extent that we *don't* believe marriage itself will save us. We are poised to live outside the roles of husbands and wives. We come from outside the straight model enough to change it, but only if we don't assimilate into it.

We can raise the standards and levels of intimacy, closeness, communication, commitment, healing, and sexuality if we know who we are and refuse to settle for the "straight" version.

Though marriage feels threatened among those who blame us, the fact is we can give it back renewed to heterosexual people as an option worth considering.

Marriage will not be for all of us. It will be just one possibility for LGBT people on the planet among numerous creative human possibilities for living and being together.

The "straight" world needs gay people to model better relationships, but not those who will ape its institutions in some hope that straight people will like them better.

Do Our Heroes Have to Be Straight-Acting?

It's finally happened. Gay men have officially arrived in the new millennium.

What convinced me was the appearance of "The First Ever Gay Men's Wedding Guide" in the August/September issue of [the now defunct] *Hero* magazine. And if *Hero* is, as its recent press release says, "the largest magazine in the U.S. for gay men," then the new millennium is most likely to be the "straightest" we've ever seen.

From its first appearance just two years ago, *Hero* has been one of the most consumer-oriented national glossies. The others are not far behind in their advocacy of conspicuous consumption as a way to save us all. But *Hero* has been playing that game much better.

Its "mainstream approach to gay life" (another quotation from its recent press release) has garnered corporate advertisers who dream of how much money they can make off of our insecurities and our discontent with ourselves. It's so much like its straight equivalents that it has been featured in the straight media. That's a clear indication of what a political statement it makes, even though it claims not to be political — wouldn't want to offend those advertisers.

It's not that the gay community shouldn't have such magazines. Let me repeat what I've said elsewhere: We have the right to all of the sicknesses and dysfunctions of the larger society. In fact, we have a lot of catching up to do so that, just like heterosexuals, we can hide our humanity behind all of the "straight-acting, straight-looking" roles that some heterosexual people today have begun to question.

Curiously missing from this "wedding" issue was that passive-aggressive phrase that usually appears on *Hero's* masthead: "The Magazine for the Rest of Us." Who are these "rest of us"? Those who don't have sex, or don't act like or admit that they do? Are they those who don't use sex for any reason other than love and commitment?

Well that can't be what its editors mean. The magazine uses sex throughout to sell itself and its products. Gay men in their underwear, without their shirts, and in provocative poses are everywhere. Every cover until the "Wedding" issue has featured the usual white males who fit the standards of male beauty that any other American magazine promotes. The ads are just as sexually oriented and use sex just as much to sell everything as those in any magazine, straight or gay. The "Wedding" issue has the first African American on the cover. He's helping a white man straighten his bow tie.

And while all of the most interesting heterosexual couples I know are designing their own ceremonies, rejecting much of the marketing that sells the things someone says everyone "needs" for that "perfect" wedding, and even questioning the state's role in relationships, not *Hero*. *Hero* promotes "Hawaii, the Ultimate Honeymoon" as well as "10 Great Honeymoon Ideas" including Bali, Paris, and Australia's Noosa.

There's a "Wedding Timeline & Planner" that recommends "Everything You Need" in order to have the perfect, white wedding. Six weeks ahead, you know, you should be designing a wedding program and having it printed.

A state-by-state guide to wedding resources tells you "everything you need to marry." There are even dieting and exercise tips with a reminder that "more pictures will be taken of you on your wedding day than probably any other time in your life." Of course, the "Timeline" says you need to book your photographer and/or videographer nine months ahead.

It was sad enough to hear a gay man say in a National Public Radio interview that with the legalization of same-sex unions in Vermont his relationship "finally felt legitimate." I had hoped that his relationship already felt that way to him for personal and self-esteem reasons.

But *Hero* has now given us the way to buy feelings of legitimacy. And, not surprisingly, we do so by looking as non-gay and as non-sexual as possible — except in the way "straight-acting" consumers already do. To be a "hero" we must exchange our ways of living sexually for the patterned ways defined by the wedding industry.

There are reasons we buy this version of living. We've been taught that the "straight" way is best and our ideas are inferior. We seek to feel okay because we don't feel legitimate without the same purchases, experiences, and products others crave.

We are ashamed of being sexual. We think that our sexuality should be in the closet. Looking and acting "straight" locks it in there deeper than heterosexual sex has ever been closeted. On top of this, we have all the fears about sexuality that straight people do and, just like them, we'd rather not face our fears either.

We believe that we can buy ourselves out of discrimination and oppression.

We think "straight" people will like us better if we act like them, and we desperately need their approval. We're ashamed of others in our community who don't act "straight" enough, men who don't look and act "manly" enough and women who aren't "feminine."

I'd certainly like to believe that we're getting healthier. I am unconvinced that *Hero* is any sign of the health of our community any more than *Glamour* and *Esquire* are signs that the straight community is healthy. And in a day when many heterosexual people are challenging the wedding industry and creating weddings that are very queer by "straight" standards, I'm struck by the fact that this largest selling gay men's magazine is hoping to make our weddings and our heros as straight as possible.

The message from corporate America is that we're just supposed to do things the way "straight" society says we should do them.

Boy, am I disappointed! All this time I'd thought the heros of gay men were supposed to be especially creative. There goes that stereotype.

The Whys of Gay Parenting

Our culture is overflowing with messages about parenting. One tells us that we're not fulfilled without having the experience of raising a child or two. And like many of the lessons we learn while we grow up, that message came from everywhere.

Our parents probably let us know that they look forward to being grandparents — I'm tickled by the bumper sticker that says, "If I'd have known how much fun grandkids are, I'd have had them first." They were also taught that children would fulfill adults. So, they passed that tip on.

Whether or not our parents would look back and say they were glad they bought into this belief, I wonder how "fulfilled" we really made them. And I am concerned about the burden it puts on most children to live with the idea that they are here to fulfill their parents.

Sometimes we wake up and realize that this is a major part of why we arrived on this planet. It might happen when we take a different path than our parents expected and we hear, "I didn't bring you up to become . . . ." Was there some unspoken contract we never realized we had agreed to just by appearing in our families?

Sometimes we see it in Little League sports. Fathers are clearly living out their own unhealed hurts around athletics when their attitude toward the umpires and referees becomes verbally, even physically, brutal. In the days when I refereed high school soccer, I remember one varsity player coming up to me during a game in response to loud yells from someone in the crowd, and saying, "I'm sorry, that's my dad."

Sometimes parental concern about their children's intimate relationships reflects more the parent's need to see that their kids have a fulfilling relationship that makes up for their own hollow marriage. They probably won't face the hollowness they feel. Some even have children in the hope that it will hold their increasingly dull relationship together.

We know that if an individual does not feel fulfilled in her or his own being, goodness, humanity, and vocation, there is no one else who can do it. In addition, when children live under the impossible burden of fulfilling their parents, they are being pressured to do something they cannot do.

Yet, children do get the message, even if it's never spoken out loud. They feel an unnamed burden upon them and are not sure what it is. They become family caretakers, stars, worriers, attention-getting rebels, and surrogate spouses. Family systems therapists see this as the "normal" pattern of families in many cultures, our's especially. And they don't believe that it's healthy for any family member in any way.

It's the unusual parent who has worked on her or his emotional image enough to have children for other reasons than self-fulfillment. As LGBT people, the culture has given us many unhealthy reasons to seek fulfillment in parenting. Our self-image has been hurt by homophobia and heterosexism. We have been told we just don't match up to cultural ideals.

So, besides the usual unhealthy messages about the fulfillment of parenting that straight people use to parent, we might feel the additional need to live up to this straight standard. The message is: parenting will make us better, like straight people. It will make us feel the fulfillment we don't have because we're not straight.

It's not that same-sex couples cannot bring up healthy children. Some studies suggest they do better than heterosexual couples.

It's not that children need both a father and a mother to be healthy. That's a popular cultural myth. If any parent is fully human, then she or he can model for a child what it is to be fully human. If a relationship is healthy, then it can model a healthy relationship. The only reason our culture claims both a man and woman are necessary, is that they can model for the children the unhealthy gender roles of "manhood" and "womanhood" on which our sexist culture thrives.

The basic question is, why do we want to be parents? Or, what are children for?

Well, they're not here to fulfill us. So, don't become parents in order to feel fulfilled. Get counseling instead. It's cheaper and less complicated.

The best reason to choose to have children is to nurture life, that is to nurture *them*, not us. Anything we get out of parenting is only a side benefit.

And when children show their own unique, disruptive-of-our-lives personalities, or go their own way, look us in the face and disagree, become right-wing bigots, give us the sense as teenagers that we are in their way, or take a career path totally against our principles, then we are being tested to see if they were here just to fulfill us.

Parents have power over children for good or ill, power to let them grow and ultimately leave to make their own way in the world. And there are so many other influences on children we can't conceive of now.

Nurturing life means saying "Hello," but it also means saying "Goodbye." It's an important, even daunting, task.

Parents will make mistakes. The better ones will admit them to their children. Children need that. They need adults who model for them how to deal with their own mistakes.

But our greatest mistake would be to become a parent to fill a hole in our own lives. That's why I like Kahlil Gibran's insightful reminder for parents: "You may give them your love, but not your thoughts."

I'd add, we better not bring them into the world so they live for us. They need to live their own lives, not ours.

Just as Good Isn't Good Enough

The American Academy of Pediatrics' endorsement and support this past month of the rights of gay men and lesbians to be parents is a prestigious validation of what we've known all along. We can be just as good at parenting as straight people.

And, we can also be just as bad.

The AAP statement is another one of those endorsements that identifies us with the same healthy, and the same sick, institutions as the rest of society. No doubt, we have the right to all of those institutions.

Not only does the AAP join the American Psychological Association and the American Academy of Child and Adolescent Psychiatry in support of lesbian and gay parenting, but it also takes a step further. The Academy calls its member doctors to become advocates for full recognition of such parenting in order to promote the health and wellbeing not of LGBT parents, but of American children.

Of course, lesbians and gay men have been parents for generations. In "don't ask, don't tell" fashion, however, their parental rights have been denied in U.S. courts with the belief that "scientific evidence" did not support their abilities. A recent Alabama example is only the latest.

Right-wing responses still cling to those old prejudices, now criticizing AAP recommendations with the same complaints they make of any professional organization that doesn't agree with their biases — that the decision was political, or under activist pressure, or based on flawed data.

Predictably, for example, Louis Sheldon, the chairman of the Traditional Values Coalition, responded to the AAP by describing what is actually a generally conservative group of physicians to the Associated Press as: "A group of pro-homosexual people...who want to further tear down the one-man, one-woman relationship in America." It's the same old rhetoric from groups whose own methods are politically heavy-handed, who are adept at using every form of activist pressure, and who cite "data" from organizations falsely self-labeled "research councils" as well as "researchers" known for skewing the results.

Of course, the support of the right of LGBT people to parent does not guarantee that LGBT people will actually be good parents any more than the right of heterosexuals to parent has guaranteed that what they do is good for their children. After all, the concept of the dysfunctional family was based on straight family models. And the generations that baby boomers complain about for the loss of morals and the destruction of whatever else they think is good, were the result of the straight parenting of baby boomers or the baby boomers' own straight parents.

The failure of the current model of a family is something that's hardly ever noticed, much less discussed, in our society. We are too stuck in this family model's patterns, too committed to its structure, too invested financially in its dysfunction. On top of this, many are too busy blaming the gains of LGBT people for the problems that a straight society and its problematic model of a family have created.

Most non-heterosexual people are too caught up in the important fight for equal rights, too quick to accept the idea that straight institutions are better, or too much in need of the approval of straight society to raise and examine the issue. Our internalized heterosexism is more likely to be enamored with straight institutions like the current nuclear family than to see the blatant and deep-rooted faults that are now pointed out by family-system therapists. Even some heterosexual parents have become concerned with rejecting such straight models for the future of their children.

Creating our families on straight models will not help children nor save LGBT people. We've got to explore what we, people who have stood outside straight culture and looked in can do to improve, heal, and break the dysfunctional patterns of the current family model.

We have no need to go into parenting as if we are the flawed ones who need to catch up to the healthy straight families. We are the ones capable of changing things for the better, because we are not straight. And we can join that small cohort of heterosexual parents who are fighting to change how our society brings up boys to be men and girls to be ladies.

We've already begun to break the limitations of the nuclear family when we've brought our friends into a child's life as non-related "aunts and uncles." We've created groups to support our parenting – straight people should have done this long ago to relieve parental stress.

Some of us will choose to nurture life directly with children whom we conceive, birth, or adopt. We need to recognize, then, that these lives are not here to be our property or one of our possessions, but lives that need to grow in their own space and time for themselves. We have chosen to help them flourish. They have not chosen us.

Some of us could choose to nurture the children who are in this world rather than think our fulfillment might lie in having children of our own. This world needs nurturing adults who supplement parents and give children the attention they need, attention that goes beyond the limitations of two adults.

All of us can refuse to limit boys by the stifling gender roles that put men out of touch with, even embarrassed by, their feelings and prepare them to be competitive warriors who can only win by defeating other men in business, sports, war, and every-day interactions. We can encourage their nurturing, peace-making, and playful qualities.

We can refuse to limit girls by the stifling gender roles that encourage them to accept chivalry rather than equal pay, teach them to sacrifice their dreams for the dreams of others, and settle for the evaluations of male-dominance. We can encourage them to define their lives for themselves and their own interests, and to develop and display their strength, insights, and wholeness.

We can emphasize alternatives to punishment, shame, and the appearance that adults know it all. We can decide to learn what children can teach us.

Of course, this all sounds pretty queer to many in our society. But that's exactly the point.

If, in spite of the dominant propaganda, we can see what LGBT people have to give to children, we'll stop aping the old tired models of parenting and find out that the alternatives are even better for children. And though some of this is already recommended by the American Academy of Pediatrics, one day they'll more fully catch up and realize all that LGBT people have to give to children.

Holidays

The Minor Details

Hey Santa, Look How
We "Good Gays" Fit In!

It happens every year — "the holiday season." It's a time we celebrate in a variety of ways, a variety of stories that hold our economy together.

Though all but the youngest of us know that "there is no Santa Claus," few retailers would deny that it's this season that keeps them in business. We all agree that Santa is mythology, but we know that such agreements are what prop up our economy. Without the myth of Santa, business would collapse. How scary would it be if we reflected too long on the idea that what we bank on is based on ideas that we agree are myths?

Even minority religious communities promote what were historically minor celebrations in their own traditions, or they add gift-giving to others. That way the season doesn't leave them behind.

Some leaders of the LGBT community argue that our economic potential is a major clue to our liberation. If those who sell things would just realize how much money we have to spend, we'd be accepted.

Those glossy national LGBT magazines that, of course, need advertising not only to survive but to make any profit, often portray us as people who "fit in" to dominant ideas of the ideal consumer. And "fitting in," looking just like "mainstream" Americans, we are often told, is what's going to win acceptance from the straight community.

We want to be loved and appreciated. We don't want to be killed, ridiculed, or isolated. But we also have been conditioned to value the ideal. We hope that finding that right partner for life, settling in a home of our own, and creating it into a castle, will save us. The only difference for LGBT people from the straight mainstream, is that we believe this not just as an ideal of "success," or as the "American dream," but as the means for survival in a hostile climate.

This image of "fitting in," of course, is usually two white males who match a mainstream Madison Avenue picture of the beautiful male model. They are strikingly healthy looking, maybe buffed, even if they may be, you know, "sick." They drink designer water and "good" wine, in their condominium or urban or suburban home, which is well-appointed with the latest electronic equipment and art, furniture, and accessories which all match, right down to the napkin holders on the dining room table. They do not watch "Roseanne" or professional wrestling, nor do they eat at McDonald's or KFC.

They are not too politically radical — they may even be Republicans, but certainly, be assured, they at least look like "mainstream" Democrats.

They're architects, writers, artists, designers, actors, or other professionals. They could be public school teachers, but certainly not assembly line workers, custodians, mechanics, or maids. And, even though we might suspect that they are sexual, these are "good gays," so that is never evident. They probably don't even think about it.

They are the gays that could live next door to us in those lily white suburbs, the gays we "live and let live" because they don't "flaunt it." These gays may even complain about those other lazy LGBT people who haven't "made it." Santa, these gays are good, for goodness sake!

This image of success, of "fitting in," is definitely "the American dream" embodied in the "middle class." And, it is classist, sexist, ageist, racist (people of color are allowed if they too "fit in" and don't "flaunt it"), able-bodyist, and, yes, homophobic.

This image has us asking ourselves and each other when we have crossed another line; when we appear to be too close openly to our own sex as well as the other sex. That's because "fitting in" really means never *acting* too "gay, lesbian, bisexual, transgender," that is "queer." In this "good gay" image, the bedroom is seldom shown, and never as a place of any activity.

Something like "marriage" for life — as close as it can be in the current legal setting — is to be assumed.

As a short-term strategy this assimilation looks good. Non-heterosexuals can hide in this. Straight people can feel that somehow their lifestyle is being affirmed by this idolizing of their straightness.

Promoting this image will remove one layer of discrimination, though not end the prejudice. It will push back into the closet not our ability to live a visible straight-acting American ideal, but certainly sexuality, for by covering LGBT people with the cloak of being "good citizens" — which means people productive to society, who fit well in appropriate patterns of consumption — it will make them look asexual.

For those who define LGBT people only in terms of their imagined bedroom activity, it will finally put that "unsightly" activity out of sight. LGBT people will get to be something that heterosexual people must be and, thus, assimilate into "the straight role."

But this unhealthy role that's conditioned into people is different from a sexual orientation. It is enforced on us with all of the means that keep any of us from stepping out of roles, from violence, to ridicule, to rejection. It keeps heterosexuals too from getting in touch with their sexuality.

It also puts us out of touch with the majority of LGBT people. Any movement that's not classist will picture the majority of its members as working class, including many people of color. ("White" is a minority color world-wide, remember.) Its images, faces, and activities will include many that are not found among LGBT images today. So, being "good gays" who fit in, will put us out of touch with the majority of the world's human population.

We will never know the variety of ways there are for us to be human, unless we develop a long-term strategy to question all the barriers that hurt us, including the conditioning to consume. And championing that variety may be one of the most appropriate responses in a season which idealizes, instead, "peace on earth and good will to (and for) all."

Family Holidays For Us

It's November and the "holiday season" again. Thanksgiving images of happy, American families gathered to celebrate love, warmth, and acceptance, surround us. They're laden with the array of consumer goods that will buy a perfect gathering and with national myths to "explain" these holidays in glowing terms.

These images set most people up for failure. They find many "celebrating" with depression and disappointment gatherings that amount to anniversaries of dysfunctional family pasts. Few actually experienced these happy, Norman-Rockwell-print gatherings. That makes *National Lampoon's Christmas Vacation* and *Home for the Holidays* sought after movie rentals this time of year.

We long for pasts that today we believe were ideal. They may never have been, for as children we didn't hear anyone talk openly about the family dynamics that were really taking place. Still, we want the people on whom we had to depend for childhood love and nurture to somehow provide the feelings now. If we are lesbian, gay, bisexual, or transgender, we want those families to love and embrace us and our identities.

Adult children are often stuck in a pattern of family expectations. Like the abused spouse who desperately holds on to the abuser, we are convinced that we can change our families to get unconditional acceptance.

We use the same excuses as the abused for hanging in there with our families: They don't really mean it. They really do love me. They said they were sorry and would be better next time. They need me. I can fix things if I just try harder. How can I survive without these people who brought me up? They're the only family I've got. I owe them so much. I don't want to hurt them.

Most of us are still carrying around dysfunctional messages from our families of origin. Many of us desperately need to fix our families. We feel that we can if we do it just right or long enough. We feel that we must change them in order to be happy ourselves.

We may live much of our life trying to do whatever it takes to get their love. It may be the main reason we waited so long to "come out," or why we're still not "out" to our family. Their approval and love is more important than our life and our loves. And we act as if we don't have the right to our own lives or loves.

Culturally, we are awash in rhetoric about the indispensability of the family of origin to our health and society. We are so conditioned to believe this, that our laws preserve the family of origin, even if by preserving it we create psychologically and physically sick members.

We believe that preserving the family of origin is so crucial that it may take the death of its children before anyone asks about a family's health. More children die in their homes in two days in America than were killed in all of 1998 in our schools.

Psychologist Alice Miller in books with titles such as *For Your Own Good: Hidden Cruelty in Child-rearing and the Roots of Violence* and *Thou Shalt Not Be Aware: Society's Betrayal of the Child*, is courageous enough to label the way we raise children "poisonous pedagogy." She identifies the fourth commandment, "Honor thy father and thy mother," as one of the most destructive in Western morality and psychology. Yet, she says, we have a difficult time admitting this, because it means we will no longer be able to deny our own past familial pain.

As LGBT people, we've got to face the fact that our happiness cannot depend on our families of origin. If we live as victims of their evaluation of us, we'll continue to live their lives, not our own.

We may have to give our families up, let them be, and face how that feels as we mourn that loss. We'll have to be clear about what we owe them and what we don't.

Parents are supposed to give their children unconditional love and nurturance, so that grown up sons and daughters can let their parents go. Parents are not supposed to make their grown-up children feel indebted for life for the job parents chose to do.

We'll have to give up attempts to change them. We'll need to set our own boundaries for what is acceptable and unacceptable behavior for our parents if they expect to be around us. And if we feel guilty when we do this, we'll need therapy and supportive groups of realistic peers.

The healthiest families are often not families of origin. They are the families we create. They include people who love us unconditionally, who listen to us closely, and who share themselves fully. These people not only care about us, but they also accept those we love.

We have every right to create these families. We have the right to invite whomever we want to join us to celebrate those holidays we choose to celebrate in the manner we choose to do so. We have the right not to act upon the objections that our families of origin raise as they try to bring us back into their agenda when we begin to live our lives on our own terms for us.

The world may call this selfish, but that is a useless message meant to stop anyone from creating their own happiness. Those who label us selfish are not those who are listening to us deeply. They are listening to the messages of their own dysfunctional families.

It's the season to create our own holiday traditions. It's the season to stop measuring our worth by how successful we are at fixing our families of origin, or by how much they accept us.

And even though they may accept us, are there others who have chosen us to love and who we this holiday season freely choose to love? Our liberation must include freedom to create relationships that nurture us, stretch us, and give us our own reasons to celebrate Thanksgiving.

'Tis the Season...

T his time of year, it's hard to ignore the religion that comes at us. Year-end religion is so necessary for a profitable U.S. retail business that it spills off the shelves onto the floors, into the streets, and all over public spaces. In addition, this year we're guaranteed that symbols of "peace on earth" will be used to promote "the war."

For those of us who continue to suffer from the spiritual abuse that our culture normally serves up, coping with this deluge of sensory stimuli can further sour us on the whole thing. "Bah, Humbug," is a more common response than our society cares to admit.

There's probably no one who has grown up in our culture who hasn't experienced spiritual abuse. There are cable channels and programs that seem sincerely devoted to it.

"Hi," the door-to-door visitors say in a religious comic strip. "We're from the church down the street and we'd like to quote the Bible to you and make you feel like dirt." And they actually call that "Good News."

Just look at how many human beings cling to the idea of hell as if it's a necessary part of their view of reality. They must want, or need, to see the world as a place where the Divine is willing to allow "his" children to suffer forever and ever, even though "he" has the power to do something about it. Any human parent who refused to stop such suffering would be separated from their children, even if the parent believed their children "deserved it."

And clever, "straight-acting" religious thinkers continue to work hard in order to justify the idea that the notion of eternal child abuse is actually compatible with a Divine Parent who is all-powerful, the epitome of justice, and unconditionally loving. The popularity of the Christian fundamentalist "Left Behind" series of novels shows how abused we've been. And arguments that there are other, less abusive, ways to interpret religious texts don't seem to cut it for many.

It's as if abuse becomes us because we are so used to it. We wouldn't know what to do otherwise. We're like the abused children and partners who return to our abusers for more because we can't live without it emotionally.

For those of us who need religion in our lives, sorting out the toxic from the healthy messages is our main task and it's often not easy. That's why counselor/minister Terry Norman's book, *Just Tell the Truth* (1998), is an insightful example of reframing the messages gay men (and others) hear when they struggle with their religious beliefs in order to attain what he calls "orientational authenticity."

For LGBT people who have found their value in religious communities, it's common to believe that the struggle between fully admitting and embracing their sexual orientation and confronting their "straight-affirming" beliefs is the Divine calling them to guilt and shame. Dr. Norman sees the truth otherwise. And we can choose to see it differently as well.

The Divine, he suggests, is actually struggling with us against those old negative, anti-gay beliefs. In reality, the struggle is Its unrelenting call to us to embrace our sexual orientation authentically, to come out.

And it's a struggle because of our lack of authenticity, because we cling to the anti-LGBT beliefs and feelings which we have so long embraced and which toxic religion wants us to promote. The Good, he asks us to consider, is really on the side of our coming out, our telling the truth. And until we do that, we'll struggle, believing it is the Divine that's holding us back while the Divine is actually prodding us to authenticity.

How we see things and frame our life is really our own choice. Affirming those old anti-LGBT beliefs has likewise really been little more than the choice of others through the ages. It's really our choice as to what we consider inspired, whether it is traditional or modern.

The historical fact is that every major religion has had times when it has oppressed LGBT people and times when it has not. Every major religion has had periods when it has affirmed individual and personal revelations as well as periods when it has been fearfully, hierarchically authoritative, denying that individual spirituality is insightful and valuable.

Past, unhealed spiritual abuse may keep us acting defensively and in anger in our inability to escape religion in the public and secular spheres this time of year. That reflects those personal issues that we have not fully dealt with regarding religion and the spiritual abuse of our pasts. It reflects our own past dashed expectations from family and faith.

Yet we can also choose to reframe this time of year, to create our own spaces and relax right in the middle of this commercial and religious blast. We can use it as a time to explore and appreciate our comfort with having no religion, or examine if religion matters to us and how and why.

When it comes to this season, we can choose what speaks to us and reject what does not.

Personally, I'm uninspired by whether the oil lamps in the Jewish Temple really remained lit or not. But Hanukkah inspires me with the message of human beings who seek their own liberation by taking charge of their destiny, and, against the greatest odds, stand up against the oppressions of their society.

Likewise, the Christmas stories often sound hokey, but I'm impressed with the ones that say the outcasts of society (like the shepherds) and the "pagan astrologers" (the Magi from the East) were the ones who got the message, while the Bible-quoting, religious rightists who preached the dominant religious understanding of the time remained clueless and hostile.

The Love of Friendship

There are shelves of books about Ms. or Mr. Right: how to get yourself ready for her or him, how to find her or him, how to keep her or him, and how to have a fulfilling relationship with her or him. There are even books about how to find the girlfriend or boyfriend within.

Some are actually very good. And they sell well, even if it seems that everything's been said at least a half-dozen times already.

Their popularity tells us how desperate we are for the right relationship with that one person who will be our intimate companion. Yet, if we took the better advice most of these books give, we'd lose that desperation. We'd begin to value ourselves as single individuals who are members of a broader community. We wouldn't think that the answer to our loneliness and feelings of incompleteness are to be found in that one husband or wife.

What's missing in this literature about relationships is how to be a friend, a real trusted, close, long-term friend. Friends just seem to be people we "have" in some casual or accidental way. We don't think about friendship in the way we analyze our relationship to a girlfriend or boyfriend.

There are times when we're really glad we have friends, and we might reflect about that. There are times when we're thankful that a friend stood by when even our coupling with a beloved fell apart. We seldom think about the love that is expressed in friendship except when other options seem to have failed us.

Culturally, we don't give much thought to deepening friendships or just being a better friend, unless it's about "winning friends" for some often unfriendly goal. Remember Dale Carnegie's *How to Win Friends and Influence People*, a book title that certainly makes friendship sound like a self-centered, profit-oriented occupation? After fifty years, it's still a top seller. But who trusts the depth of commitment of any salesperson who wants you to feel like their friend?

Real, deep friendship isn't a model of relating that's sellable. It makes little money for anyone in comparison to the profits of selling that one beloved who could be our partner, husband, or wife.

After a study of the literature on business, Sam Keen writes in *Fire in the Belly: On Being a Man* (1992) that this lack of emphasis upon friendship relates to the nature of masculine models of doing business today. There is not, he notes, a single chapter on friendship in all the books on business. It's not a part of good business anymore. And the higher one rises in a corporation, the less one is friends with the majority of its employees. As Keen puts it: "Nobody hugs the boss."

Though the grown-up preoccupation is to make Valentine's Day a time to celebrate the one beloved we're lucky to have in our lives, or to bemoan the lack thereof, it wasn't always that way. As children, before all the conditioning about needing a man or woman to fulfil us took hold, Valentine's Day was a chance to think of friends.

In the days of passing out those tiny little valentines in early elementary school, we weren't thinking of giving them only to that special one. In fact, we might have been told that the rule was everyone in class gets a valentine. There was an expectation that being someone's valentine had to do with good friendship. And it was easier to say, "I love you" to a friend, or hold hands, or put your arm around someone without worrying about how that would be taken or what that might mean beyond a friendship that embodied what then seemed to be a natural human closeness.

There's actually a large body of literature in the traditions of both the East and the West that celebrates good friends. It was easier to express the love that was friendship in societies and at times when homophobia was less rampant. Without that fear of getting close to one's own sex, no one had to worry about whether a relationship was too close, too intimate, and too cherished.

And when same-sex sexual activity was less an issue, it was easier to be closer to friends of the same sex, and even to express that friendship in romantic terms. David and Jonathan in the Hebrew Bible could swear allegiance to each other, make a "covenant" to each other, and "love" each other, as David described it, "more than the love of women." Jesus of Nazareth could have one disciple "whom he loved," and could allow that disciple to lay his head on his chest. Again in the Hebrew Bible, Naomi and Ruth could commit themselves to each other forever without question.

All of these people had same-sex relationships. And friendship can be one kind of same-sex relationship.

But to us, the cultural emphasis on sexual and romantic coupling and its anti-gay prejudice has even made the phrase "same-sex relationships" sound like it only refers to relationships that are sexual. The fact is, we do not know whether many of these close relationships in the past were sexual or not. But the interest in proving it one way or the other is a result of our culture's homophobia. Otherwise, it wouldn't be an issue at all.

Down through history there are numerous examples of close friendships. But the negative attitudes and oppression of LGBT people make such closeness difficult today because it labels it "gay." Internalized homophobia causes us to wonder "what this means." And as long as it's considered bad to be gay, the fear that such close friendships might mean "I'm gay" keeps them from developing.

In addition, when a culture defines closeness in sexual terms, then as a friendship gets closer, the issue of sexual activity complicates closeness. For some people, closeness is only expressed in sexuality. For others, closeness is only experienced in sexuality. And the movie *When Harry Met Sally* concluded that men and women cannot "merely" be friends. Sex must be involved when people are that close.

Closeness and love are parts of deep friendships. They are expressed in the many ways closeness can be expressed. And close friends listen carefully, affirm one's value, stand by in thick or thin, and support personal growth. They are not only gifts of the universe but relationships that do need attention, development, and celebration.

Histories

The Minor Details

Getting Over Our Amnesia

A group without knowledge of its history is like a human being with amnesia. They don't know who they are or where they are in the larger scheme of things. People of color know this, and that's why they believe in the importance of understanding and teaching the history that's been left out of official and approved history books.

As Gay and Lesbian History Month, October is not only a chance to find heros and heroines throughout history who are like us, but a time to remember where we are on the timeline that chronicles LGBT events. Just as it has been a struggle to include the histories of other minority groups and women in the public consciousness, so is it with the histories of our communities. The straight world has a stake in burying our histories as "unimportant, insignificant, partisan, politicized, and deviant," for that burial keeps us victims.

There are things even we do to live a life of amnesia and suffer its consequences. When a generation of LGBT people doesn't know what has gone before it, it's easy, on the one hand, to live as if there is little hope for real and radical change.

This feeling of hopelessness on our part is a prerequisite for maintaining the status quo. It prevents us from realizing what actual and basic changes have taken place, even those that mark how different things are today from just ten or twenty years ago.

An older friend of mine tells of the buses that would pull up to gay bars to haul everyone off to jail. Another tells of churches that are now open and accepting when just ten years ago they were closed and condemning. Another tells about the struggle the difficult struggle with many temporary setbacks, less than ten years ago, that resulted in "sexual orientation" being added to a city's human rights ordinance.

If we don't know these stories, we may think that there is little hope for change today because we won't remember what changes have taken place. And without hope we become tentative, afraid, and conservative. We prefer to blend in, accept any crumbs of tolerance we have been given, be left alone, hide in dysfunctional huddling together to protect us from the dangerous world out there, or buy our safety and security by becoming model consumers.

Without hope we become too afraid to take the chance of showing our love in public, kissing our partner goodbye, or holding their hand. We're afraid we might get hurt. We might be critical of others who do and might resurrect conservative moralisms to support our criticisms. We might criticize same-sex public affection of this sort in a way that we would never criticize similar, every-day heterosexual expression. And we might really be afraid that "calling attention to it" will bring criticism upon us.

To know our history is to know how far we've come. It is to know that just as those before us have made it better for us, we do not have to settle for this. We can make it even better.

To know our history is to know that it really was a struggle to get here, sometimes at great cost and against seemingly insurmountable odds. It was not a straight line of progress, but two steps forward and one step, sometimes two steps, back, of lost battles, persistent pressure, and "obnoxious" leaders who, by not giving in and not giving up, scared the powers that be so that "moderates" would be heard and even heeded.

To know our history is to know that our own actions will not be in vain, no matter how hopeless it feels, and no matter how small they seem to be. It shows, as U.S. historian Howard Zinn says, that ". . . no pitifully small picket line, no poorly attended meeting, no tossing out of an idea to an audience or even to an individual should be scorned as insignificant." (*You Can't Me Neutral on a Moving Train: A Personal History of Our Times*, 1994)

On the other hand, not knowing our history can lead us to believe that there is no need for further activism, that we have arrived in the "Promised Land." We can feel as if we have somehow made it and that our freedoms are forever secure.

Our history tells us, however, that it was "not so long ago" that we did not have the freedoms we do now. They must be maintained, for as the saying goes, "the price of freedom is constant vigilance."

Partying on at the club, criticizing those who are activists, failing to see the relationship between the issues of transgender people and gay men, lesbians, and bisexual people, buying into the dominant belief that there is no relationship between today's version of a conservative economic agenda and discrimination against those who don't act American (still defined as straight, white, masculine, and upper class) enough, are clues that we don't remember or that we have the selective memory encouraged by the dominant view.

Knowing our history reminds us how much better things could still be, because those in our past who fought for what we now have would not settle for anything less than everything.

As one older friend reminded me, "Though we did not know how, and though we did not know what it all meant, we knew back then that we would never stop until our love was not just tolerated but celebrated like the love of everyone else. We didn't think that was too much to ask. I still don't think so."

Our history reminds us that this is no time to give up that dream.

A Lesson from Stonewall

I know that the excitement that began in the early morning hours of June 28, 1969 outside a Greenwich Village gay bar called the Stonewall Inn really isn't the historical beginning of the movement for LGBT rights.

The 1950's saw the founding of organizations such as the Daughters of Bilitis, ONE, Inc., and the Mattachine Society. In the fifties, gay people also began to turn to the courts to fight for the right to receive gay magazines in the mail or to congregate in bars without police harassment.

But the civil disturbances that came to be called the "Stonewall Riots" appeal to me symbolically the way the Battle of Bunker Hill or Paul Revere's late night ride symbolize the beginnings of the American Revolution. It makes one proud to identify with a legacy which says "Enough is enough," or, as Popeye would put it, "That's all I can stands 'cuz I can't stands no more."

Was that night at Stonewall disorderly? You bet.

The order of things was bigoted, harassing, and deadly. When people oppose the order of things, the keepers of the status quo accuse them of disorderly conduct. So, to be "orderly" is not a neutral, non-political act. It promotes the skewed values and "normal" discrimination of the current structures.

Was it messy? It sure was.

Real healing makes messes. In fact, democracy itself is messy. It's not for neat freaks or the anal-retentive. It's not for those who want to look good in the eyes of those who set the dominant, sick agenda and who reward anyone who supports it.

Was it perfect? I doubt it. And, actually, I hope not.

Much has been lost in the struggle for freedom by those who wait for things to be done perfectly. It was a hot, muggy night of spontaneous resistance, the kind that explodes out of a long lasting, wearing, burden of oppression that the larger community refuses to acknowledge.

Was it led by gay leaders who worried about what straight people would think of them if they didn't remain moderate, middle-of-the-road, "straight-acting," and nice? Of course not.

If any worried mainline gay leaders were in the bars that night, they didn't want to stand out. They probably even criticized these radicals as ignorant rabble.

Did it take place in the boardroom, the theater, a concert hall, a dinner party, or a fine, well-mannered social club? Are you kidding?

The Stonewall Inn (next door to the present New York bar by that name) was a shabby dive that served watered-down drinks in glasses that were questionably sanitary. It wasn't really even a drag queen's bar. Only a certain number of drag queens were allowed in at a time and only if they were known by the owners.

Was it led by gay leaders who drank expensive wine, read best-selling books, could afford to attend expensive fund-raisers, hob-knobbed with politicians, and invested wisely? No.

As if to throw the whole issue of LGBT classism in our faces, it was led by drag queens and street people. I hope that it will forever be recognized that the symbol of our liberation is not the cultured and coiffed but the least understood and the down on their luck. They were the people looked down upon by others as lazy, dirty, and "low class."

But that's not how the real combatants saw the scene. The late Ray "Sylvia Lee" Rivera, who remembered she was dressed fabulously that night, recalled that to be there in the midst of the mess and disorder of the Stonewall revolution was "beautiful and exciting":

"I'm glad I was in the Stonewall riot. I remember when someone threw a Molotov cocktail, I thought, 'My god, the revolution is here. The revolution is finally here.' . . . I just knew that we would fight back. I just didn't know it would be that night. I'm proud of myself as being there that night. If I had lost that moment, I would have been kinda hurt because that's when I saw the world change for me and my people." (In Leslie Feinberg, *Trans Liberation*, 1998, 109)

There are people who don't find drag shows entertaining, but to have the symbol of gay liberation as the resistance of drag queens and street people reminds us of what's important. It's not the ability to fit in, to rest in comfort, and to gain the approval of the powers that be. It's the prophetic disturbance by the outcasts of society. And Stonewall also symbolizes our connection to the other human issues they represent: poverty, gender oppression, and racism.

Was it non-violent? Hardly. For one committed to non-violence, it's hard to face that fact.

That the United States was born in violence and symbolizes its birth violently, probably contributes to the violent nature of our country. At least, our leaders like to use those images to justify our emphasis on the symbols, mythology, and responses of war and our war-dependent economic machine.

I'd still like to believe that we could change things non-violently — though certainly not passively. I also understand that when people have been oppressed long enough, and when other attempts to get society to focus attention on their need for humane treatment have raised no interest, then the volume of the cry for relief increases, and the methods used escalate and break out in direct confrontation.

And when I hear LGBT leadership collude with the structures by saying, "Just calm down and relax. Don't get worked up over it," then I know that such leadership is out of touch with the sufferings of its people.

So when I read the Executive Director of the Log Cabin Republicans, Rich Tafel, argue that there is no need for the federal government to enact the Employment Non-Discrimination Act to ban employment discrimination based on sexual orientation, I knew that he had to be a well-off, white male who is out of touch with the majority of LGBT people. Tafel has aligned with people who put their hope in salvation by the corporate-run order. He's aligned with politicians who prefer to deny the existence and humanity of street people and discrimination of all sorts, people who support government regulation and control only when it benefits them. Why should government tell employers to end discrimination when well-off gay people already feel free from it?

Tafel's statements are far from the tradition expressed by the Stonewall combatants. He doesn't seem to understand what the history of human liberation is about. But then, he's not really one of those who would have been caught up in the fight at Stonewall that night.

Being a Gay Patriot

July fourth. It's U.S. Independence Day. But what does a day labelled "Independence" mean to people who have never been fully free?

Howard Zinn, the historian and author of the important *A People's History of the United States* (One of those books I wish everyone would read, so we all started on the same page.) is often asked how he can be patriotic when his works have opened American history to the truth of what was really going on among America's people: the poor, women, Native Americans, other people of color, immigrants, and gays.

People come away from Zinn's writings angered, shocked, depressed, and hopeless, even though he intends to show how hopeful things are. In addition, he concludes, contrary to what we've been taught to believe, the real hope of these fifty states has always been found in the capable hands of everyday people, not presidents, congressmen, and other so-called "leaders."

Zinn's answer is that patriotism is not loyalty to the country's institutions but to its people, not to the nation in some blind, abstract sense, but to the citizens who in their daily lives push national leaders to be more and more human.

It's loyalty to a constitution and laws that are fluid, not really set in stone for those "strict constructionists" who want no change.

After all, the original constitution was only for landed, white males. They alone were treated as full human beings; only they had the right to vote. It took generations before white women and people of color could vote. It took even longer before poll taxes and restrictive tests were eliminated so that anyone regardless of color and class could actually vote.

And every stage in the process was accompanied by naysayers who believed the country would fall apart because of it. These conservatives claimed that this "Roman Empire" too would come crashing down around us in chaos and immorality if the vote came to the less worthy beings that had been left out. The Electoral College that really elects our President is still a remnant of the fact that these forefathers did not trust us everyday people who might demand an equality of treatment and respect preserved only for rich, white, men.

So, as we struggle for our rights, for the simply equal status that people perceived to be heterosexual have, we hear the same old responses that have rung throughout American history. Equality for us will destroy religion, society, the family, and children, and who knows what else. And the similarity of these warnings reminds us that the issue is not us, not who we are, not our sexual orientation.

The issue is the systemic and institutionalized prejudice, bigotry, and scapegoating, that has been a dynamic of American history since the persecutions of Baptists, Catholics, the Irish, Quakers, Jews and others in the original thirteen colonies. There's a long history of discrimination and oppression in America and it isn't pretty. There are countless Matthew Shepherds among all of the victimized groups.

What's changed all this, what's responsible for real progress — in fact for all progressive change in America — is not presidents and the bland, hopefully inoffensive, so-called national leaders we elect every so many years. It's every-day people who were fed up and as a result just decided to change things. They pressured the powers to change.

Our official history books want us to believe it's because of the great heros, people who are not like us, but better, wiser, stronger, more talented, born at the "right" place or time, or made of a better kind of stuff. Zinn's writings show us this is just not true. It's part of that false mythology we learned in school. And believing it keeps us hopeless.

Change is taking place today as it has for the two hundred and twenty-three years since the Declaration of Independence intended that all white, landed males would be free. And the movement for equal rights for lesbians, gay men, and bisexual and transgender people, is making progress. The greatest proof of that is how scared and reactive the old guard is.

But that progress depends on us each doing the small tasks we do right where we are. It's not the great heros of fashion, entertainment, politics, and corporate America featured in the gay versions of *People* magazine, who will make permanent change in this land, though I am thankful for all of them, and they might even inspire the rest of us. But their stories are false if they lead us to think that these are the kind of people who are needed to change things and that we have nothing to add to the people who make these glossy pages.

History tells us, Zinn says, that progressive change comes from people like us who decide that they've had enough, that they're not going to take it any more.

They'll write letters, march anonymously in parades, stuff envelopes for our causes, comfort the worn-out public leaders among us, push the agenda in their churches, civic groups, unions, political caucuses, workplaces, schools and colleges, and contribute a dollar or two here and there to causes that make sense to them.

We've all met these people. They're inspiring. They'll never get an award, hardly ever hear a "Thank you," or never be listed among the top people of our movements. But they make me a patriot. They're the reason this country is here and they're the future of any country that's really people-oriented.

And all they want is real independence. They know down deep that "Nobody's free, until everybody's free."

What's Tradition For?

I think it was a French skeptic who observed: "History is just one damn thing after another." And Henry Ford agreed: "History is bunk."

Not true. We need to know our history in order to see how much more is possible and to be aware of all that has been accomplished by our predecessors. History tells us how we got to this place, for better or for worse, and whether we're stuck here or not (Usually not.).

But in what sense does history somehow provide us with our norms, tell us how things should be, or model what must be done? And are we somehow victims of our past?

Those are questions we need to ask when we hear someone use that loaded word: "tradition." That's because the basic issue is: just because something is traditional, does that make it good, moral, humane, just, caring, or even valuable enough to preserve?

Now, a lot of things are traditional because they've made it down through history, sometimes against apparently overwhelming odds. Slavery is traditional. Women idealized as male property is traditional. Living with cockroaches is traditional. So are an assortment of diseases such as small pox, typhoid, and pneumonia. To fight them is to go against the weight of tradition.

Yet often "It's traditional" has been evoked to claim that certain things shouldn't change, as if we are expected to assume that because something is traditional it's better than things that aren't. "Love one another" is a traditional recommendation, but its value doesn't rest in the fact that it's an old idea, and certainly not in whether or not it's traditionally been widely practiced.

That something is "traditional" has been used to argue against LGBT people just as it has against any group that a dominant culture has historically marginalized. If one thing is surely traditional, it's discrimination.

"Traditional family values," seems to refer to the values of white, patriarchal, punishment-oriented, middle-class families of the 1950's. Those values are supposed to be better than treating women and children as full human beings who are as good as grown-up males, or recognizing the value of letting people love whomever they choose.

"Traditional understandings of the Bible" are assumed to be better than those of modern scholarship, especially if they are taken to condemn anything that threatens "traditional family values." Words like "revisionism" and "modernism" are used as put downs. And this is so even if these "traditional" interpretations actually were developed as late as the mid-twentieth century.

Religious traditions are defined by authorities who see themselves as somehow more qualified than the rest of us to tell us how things should be. They actually include only a small number of the ideas, events, and morals from religious history while they ignore many others. Then these traditions are used to tell people who they are and confine them inside internalized, restrictive psychological, emotional, and social boundaries that promote guilt, condemnation, and self-hate in those, often LGBT people, who don't fit in.

It's the emotional attachment to a tradition that imprisons. We were not taught that a tradition is valuable and true merely through logical discussions of it with us. Traditions were given to us as members of a community, which may have included our immediate families — a community that defined us, accepted us, affirmed us, and validated us. We learned that that community would do so until we stepped outside of its "traditional" beliefs to live on our terms for ourselves.

As LGBT people come out to themselves and the world about them, their attachment to these communities and their way of seeing things is emotionally difficult to sever. They find themselves putting much of their emotional energy in relating to, arguing against, or obsessing over these traditions even if the traditions actually invalidate LGBT people. Those outside a tradition can be baffled by why the stuck ones just can't get over it.

So, who chooses which of the array of events of the past are to be considered traditions, that is, which events are more than just past happenings? Someone had to decide which of history's events and ideas provide norms for the present and which do not.

All traditions have been defined by someone or some group who picked and chose a few things from the treasure-trove that is the past. Otherwise everything that's ever happened or been said would be included in every tradition.

And all traditional ideas and norms at one time weren't traditional. They were brand new at the time. They began as something other than what was then traditional.

So who says that you and I can't define today for ourselves what is a part of our tradition and what isn't? And what loss, abandonment, fear, guilt, and emptiness would we feel if what we chose was different from that of our parents, our religious communities, or other cultural institutions? That's for us to decide.

Though we may believe the voices that say we can't, shouldn't, or aren't able to do so, the fact is, we are fully capable of choosing for ourselves. It's a decision we can make. It's our choice to make and define our own traditions. It's also our choice whether or not to be a part of the traditions defined by others.

A refreshing new book coauthored by L. William Countryman and M.R. Ritley entitled *Gifted by Otherness* (2001) is must reading for any LGBT person who still wants to remain a part of "the Christian tradition." It's a model of no longer living as LGBT victims of what people claim is Christianity.

We aren't victims of anyone else's definitions or traditions. We don't need to live under the belief that we are only worthy human beings when others who hide behind tradition will love us.

We can be as innovative as we want. We can choose what to value. We can choose what ideas and beliefs will define us. We can choose not to be victims of "tradition" any longer.

Leadership

The Minor Details

Leading the Really Proud

It's "Pride Month" in recognition of those drag queens who in June 1969 refused to be victimized any longer by the police at the Stonewall Inn in Greenwich Village. That inelegant, disorderly "resistance" came to symbolize the beginning of the modern human rights movement.

Today "pride" festivals take place all over the country, and, for most gay, lesbian, bisexual, and transgender people, these events are a chance to party, to celebrate what it means to be part of a "queer" minority with a long history of victimization and denigration.

For the partiers it's a day or two of revelry.

For the organizers who worked to make them happen — at times it must have seemed to be against all odds — it's the result of months of preparations and planning. Think of permits, parade logistics, fund-raising, appeasing the various factions of the community or ticking them off, contradicting the naysayers, following ideas that led to dead ends, seeing to it that a plethora of volunteers followed up on their promises, filling in when they didn't, arguing with members of their boards, begging to get the support of other organizations, paying bills, ordering tee-shirts, securing vendors and local and national financial support, bargaining with entertainers and their agents, being on the scene during the event to take care of unforeseen lapses, etc., etc.

I have never organized such an event, though I have attended many and had the honor of speaking at a few. I can only imagine the enormity of their volunteer effort that pays off for all of us while it often drains them of energy for months or years to follow.

And the leaders whom I have met, have put the interests of the community at heart. They have been good people who have acted upon their own pride in the belief that we all need a chance to celebrate what too many have had to hide for so long.

Yet, we find other vocal members of our community not assuming the best of our leaders in this and other efforts, but taking aim from the sidelines, criticizing both the events and the leaders. Often the critics are from other LGBT organizations who are not content to be happy that something is happening at all and someone has volunteered to make it happen. They not only push advice but criticize the leaders', often merely assumed, motives and methods. The rumors fly and the negative ones are spread without ever approaching the leadership personally to sort things out in good faith.

There are the people who want every event to play well to the heterosexual community in the hope of greater acceptance.

There are those who want their own political, social or entertainment issue covered on every occasion.

There are those who merely assume, in that very American fashion, that anyone who leads has suspect motives and uses compromised methods.

There are people who feel "left out" because they were never asked to help, but they never volunteered in the sustained manner over-stressed leaders need to hear in order to get an over-worked leader's very divided attention.

There are others who are burned out from criticisms of their own past leadership and who still need to play their disappointments and bitterness out on current leaders.

One could go on. But the dynamic here is common.

Groups that have been victimized by the larger society, devour their leaders. It's part of the victim role society teaches us to act out. It helps maintain divisions that keep us victims by preventing concerted, unified action.

As long as we fight openly over techniques, strategies, philosophies and motives, there will be little progress. The oppression will grind on.

And have you noticed that it's easier, with fewer societal penalties, to attack the leaders of one's community than to work to end the causes of the systemic oppression around us? Minority communities know the greater dangers of attacking the dominant community when compared with the ease of destroying one's own.

So, what can we do to step out of this victim role?

First, leaders have got to be clear about why they are leading. The healthiest reason is actually not so that they will do something for an LGBT community from which they will receive thanks. Accolades are wonderful, but they are harder to come by from oppressed groups.

Leaders lead because they want to end what is hurting *them*. And if they end what is hurting them, we will all benefit. There is no selfishness in this motive, though we have been brought up to feel there is and that our real worth is in sacrificing ourselves for others. Leaders need to see how what they do brings personal benefit, for we recognize that individual humans and groups heal by ending what is hurting them. Taking leadership is stepping out of the victim role to do something to end our hurting.

Leaders need to recognize that the groups they lead are most often the least able to provide them with support around leadership — especially groups conditioned into the victim role. So, leaders need to create support elsewhere as safe places to vent the frustrations and pursue the dreams of leadership. Otherwise, they will burn out, if they aren't blown out first.

The rest of us have to deal with the issues that we play out on anyone who tries to lead. Our personal and community's health require that we heal from the effects of past hurts that reappear in our treatment of our present leaders.

What are the hurts and messages that we still carry from authority figures in the past and we project on leaders in the present? What keeps us from assuming the best of our leaders until there is real evidence otherwise? Why do we readily believe the ugly rumors? Why do we feel that when others lead it's somehow at our expense?

Pride in ourselves and our community is wrapped up in our pride in each other, no matter how imperfect, inelegant, and even bumbling are our attempts. They may be just as imperfect and inelegant as actions of those who led the wild events at Stonewall that we celebrate.

Pride also includes celebrating those who, given what they have had to work with, have done the best anyone most likely could have done to enable us to celebrate who we are, and to celebrate that even inelegantly and imperfectly.

What Is it About Pride Festivals?

There was something about the Street Festival that accompanied April's Millennium March on Washington that I really liked. It's the same thing I like about the Pride Festivals that often take place in June.

It certainly wasn't our bickering about the purpose, the process, the procedures, and the politics of a festival — which you can guarantee will be part of most pridefests. It wasn't the inability of those of us who aren't doing anything to improve them ourselves to just be happy that someone is doing something. It wasn't just that for many of us it was another chance to promote drunkenness in our community, as if we needed excuses for self-abuse. It wasn't even the fact that there were questionable money practices by some people at some times. We are now hearing those reports about the Millennium Festival.

So, what is it that I like personally? I think it's actually the carnival or state fair atmosphere. That's how the Millennium Festival struck me.

There was dancing and music, and people who usually don't come out for such "out" things. There were booths selling souvenirs and food and our slick national magazines. A few booths were even political, or service-oriented. I do like learning about our organizations at pridefests, and hope that those groups with limited budgets (the Human Rights Campaign booth appears not to be very limited) can afford booths.

I've met some people who are "above" attending such events for the very reason that I like them. Pridefests are too plebeian for them, too populated by us commoners — unlike the opera, gala openings, and fashionable, high-priced AIDS fund raisers most of us can't afford. I suppose they'll never know or care about what they're missing, but I wouldn't miss it for the world.

I regret that some pridefests are pricing themselves out of reach for many in our community who have told me that for that reason they quit attending. I would hate to hear that the goal of its organizers was actually to keep working class people away. If portions of our community are left out because of the cost of national personalities or "prime" locations, none of that is worth missing the variety of people who would otherwise attend. I'd rather showcase all the local acts of our community in a park setting. Even with corporate sponsors some pridefests have not managed to remain free.

I think it's the grass roots nature of the smaller mid-America fests that I like. They actually include rallies to remind us that we haven't "made it" yet. But then again maybe the people who don't attend because they are "above" such things, feel they have made it.

I like the broad community base of support in some festivals. I like meeting old friends and making new ones at real picnics.

The festivals are perfect places for people watching, and I like the variety of us who appear. There is something about the chance to see who makes up our strange community and its supporters. And it's fun to see the most outrageous. No matter what their personal, psychological agendas might be, I like them. They represent something too important for us to lose — if we can open ourselves to it.

Those of us concerned for "good press" in the straight community, and not "giving excuses" for right-wing criticism, must hate it. But there is something about the desire to transgress that up-tight, gender-conditioned, limited, superficially healthy, outwardly moralistic, institutionally promoted, military-prison-corporation complex defined, consumer-oriented, straight role that makes me smile.

There are people who show off everything they can get away with and maybe more than others would like to see. There are people in drag who may be hiding much of themselves so they can express something else. There are men with health club made muscles who are showing us the armor that protects them from vulnerability. There's leather, camp, piercings, jest, and butch and fem. There are critics of the transgressors. There are people dressed to kill by Abercrombie and Fitch. There are people who "flaunt it" and others who hate that "they have to flaunt it."

But that's exactly what I like. And I don't care what the "straight" community says. If up-tight straight people want to pick on us, they'll do it no matter what we do.

Of course there are gay people who think that if we live in the dominant straight image, we'll be really loved unconditionally by straight people They don't seem to notice that the real condition for straight people tolerating us is that we ape straight dysfunctions..

I don't necessarily identify with all that I see. Who does? I don't identify with straight Mardi Gras either. But I get a kick out of seeing it.

I like how it challenges me — and in the long run challenges everyone — to ask "Why?" "Who says?" and "What's really going on here?" We're no healthier than the "straight" community and it's very sick. So the answer for all of us may just be how we can be different, not how "straight" we look.

So, bring on the festivals and fairs. Let's celebrate our diversity while we work to change the most up-tight culture that ever existed on the planet. Fun and the struggle for liberation can go together. And having fun while being proud is a political act defying those who think we should be miserable because we're not "straight" like them.

The Hazards of Leading Us

It's predictable. If you ever try to do anything that might be seen as leadership in LGBT communities, you're going to be ridiculed, accused of all sorts of evil motives, and just plain attacked. And it's most likely to happen in the most public of forums.

Have you tried to lead a pride festival? Well, you haven't done it right. Tried to edit a newsletter or magazine? You're over-using your power. Stood up to find yourself the public spokesperson for a cause? You aren't qualified to speak for us. Started a movement? You don't even have yourself together.

Your motives are suspect. Your income is ill-gotten. Your personal life disqualifies you. Your ego is too big. (Imagine, thinking *you* can improve things!) You must have something to hide. You've stolen some of your ideas. You've left someone out. You're making "straight" people like us less or criticize us more. You're taking too long or moving too quickly. You've failed.

We do this. We do it often, and many of us seem to find our emotional stride in doing this. We take on an air of righteous indignation when we do. This negative crusade becomes our life instead of creating positive alternatives.

It's classic victim role activity. Any group that has been victimized by the larger society is also taught to live as victims. Since taking on the dominant group might bring more oppression, or at least make the dominant group like us less — and the victim role teaches us to live so that they will really like us and validate us — it's easier to pick on each other and eat our own.

Instead of assuming the best of our leaders, we're taught to jump on every flaw, point out when they haven't done it eloquently enough, and end up destroying what could have been good for all of us. I've seen it happen over and over — to churches, bookstores, magazines, projects, community centers, and movements that were standing up for us against larger cultural forces.

It especially seems to happen when an organization, group, or movement is at its prime, or just about to make a breakthrough. Criticisms of leadership then emerge to defuse energies, destroy loyalties, and even cause the collapse of what are important alternative institutions.

It's the reason I recommend to anyone that tries to lead that they do so for what they personally will get out of it. Forget the idea that this thought is selfish. Leadership begins when *you* see a need to end something that is hurting *you*. That's because ending what's hurting you as a human being will benefit everyone.

If I lead to help those other people, I might feel quite charitable for a while, even energized. But I'll soon learn that victimized people seldom have much personal space to say thank you. They're still fighting their own external and internal oppression.

Our communities have so much healing of their personal hurts to do, that they have a hard time accepting what is done at face value. They've been so hurt by the motives and actions of others that they begin with the expectation that this will be more of the same. And, even more than most Americans, they have a difficult time beginning with the assumption that people who lead, and seem to do so successfully, have good intentions, are trying their best, *and* will make mistakes.

The first thing someone living in the victim role does when there appears to be some problem with the activities of a leader, is what psychologists call "triangulation." Instead of going directly to leaders and asking them what they meant to do, assuming they meant well, the victim role finds others to discuss the issue with and agree with them that the leader has done something evil.

Having a pack of others gives one courage, validates one's stance, and creates a whole group of people who get along because they have in common the fact that they haven't gone directly to talk with the leader. Assuming the leader's motives were bad from the start becomes the group's view of reality, and attacking the leader becomes the reason for group loyalty.

It's all very tacky. It's all very common. And it's living as victims of the leadership and the larger societal oppression. We have to change *them*, the leaders, before *we* can be right.

What would all this be like if we didn't begin by acting out of our conditioned victim role?

First, we would be facing, not denying, our own internal issues so we were not acting out of our past hurts. When we can take a relaxed, learning stance toward things, instead of reacting, even over-reacting, to others, and when we can assume the best of our leaders until we have spoken with them, we will not be living as victims who are reacting to what leaders do.

Second, we can assume the best of our leaders until we have *personally* heard their side of the story. When we don't assume the best, we are reacting to our own past experiences, not present realities. We react negatively to protect ourselves because we don't want to be hurt, ridiculed, abandoned, or have our hopes destroyed again. Assuming they will again disappoint or hurt us now, we don't go to the leaders asking, "Help me understand this." We've already made our judgments.

Third, we will allow our leaders to make mistakes. If we expect our leaders to wait till they will do something perfectly, we'll get nothing done. As Melody Beattie, the author of numerous books on codependency, puts it: "Perfectionism leads to procrastination, leads to paralysis." In most cases, something done ineloquently is actually better than nothing.

Fourth, we would always follow with the next thought: What can I do to make this better? Should I offer to help? Should I offer other support to the over-worked? Should I begin my own movement to provide an alternative but not one motivated by just being against the other? .

We can step out of the victim role to use our energies to end the oppression of LGBT people or we can fight among ourselves while the same old society grinds on. It's our choice. Besides, by choosing to change our attitudes toward our leaders we could actually be supporting them to lead us more effectively. And isn't that our goal?

.

It Happened in Topeka, Kansas

Nationally, all that most people know about Topeka, Kansas is that it's the home of the notorious Fred Phelps clan. Phelps is the disbarred Kansas attorney who gathered a group of family members around him to form the Westboro Baptist Church and to ordain him their minister.

Phelps came upon a way to gain attention for himself and his tiny family affair, all in the name of God. He would picket the funerals of AIDS victims using the most outrageous, attention-getting signs and taunts.

As this wore thin on the local scene, he took his attention-seeking crusade nationally to funerals such as Randy Shilts' and Matthew Shepherd's. For more airtime he added other events, demonstrating at a variety of political and entertainment gatherings.

Just as the drug addict needs more and stronger fixes, the Phelps gang needed more shocking signs and hateful taunts to stay in the national spotlight. Since the media are quite fickle, the Phelps clan also needed new venues to haunt and bigger personalities who were more mainstream to picket.

Now, Topeka is a small city in the middle of the American heartland. In some ways it represents many American cities and towns. It's conservative, cautious, and convinced that the greatest compliment that one can pay any group of people is: "They blend in." That means citizens don't call attention to themselves or that they allow people to think that the straight, white, male is the norm everyone in town adores and follows.

In addition, Topeka is the capital of a state that has basically been taken over by religious and political right-wing extremists who would like nothing better than to have evolution thrown out of the public schools, abortion inaccessible to women, and LGBT people available as handy objects for discrimination. One female state legislator is even on record wishing that women didn't have the vote. Most Democratic politicians in Kansas would qualify as Republican conservatives and moderates in many other states.

Topeka isn't the Big Apple, the City by the Bay, West Hollywood, P-town, or the Big Easy. It's one of those towns LGBT people flee from and often use as the butt of their jokes. It's easy to give up on such places and write them off as lost.

But Topeka, Kansas is also the home of a small and growing band of activists who decided more than a decade ago to change the climate of oppression against LGBT people in their hometown. They are lesbian, gay, bisexual, and transgender people, PFLAG parents and friends, and a growing list of progressive allies. They're leaders who have worked through a series of organizations to produce rallies, pride festivals, pride parades, demonstrations, and political activities. And slowly and painfully they've made progress.

They've had to fight the right wing every step of the way. They've encountered conservative, homophobic religious groups who opposed them but felt even more righteous about their bigotry because they weren't as hateful-looking as the Phelps clan. They've fought and influenced a daily newspaper that preferred to ignore them. They've encountered city and county leaders who would rather grandstand or hide than consider the issue. They've pushed, been defeated, and pushed again.

On September 10, 2002, the Topeka City Council, with a loud group of 600 outside representing all views on the issue, adopted an ordinance making it unlawful to commit certain crimes motivated by intimidation or bias, and the ordinance included "sexual orientation." The evening was mixed, for "gender identity or expression" was removed from the proposal that had been submitted by four of the council members. In addition, a close 5-4 vote rejected a second ordinance which would have included sexual orientation and gender identity or expression in the city's nondiscrimination policy.

The tired group who worked to accomplish more was disappointed. Who could blame them? Their goals for that late summer evening were much higher. Many might have been tempted to give up, to consider this September 2002 outcome a failure. After all, they could say, this is the conservative heartland.

And yet, against great odds, they had moved their conservative community forward. Certainly, discrimination is still legal in Topeka, but there are now legally-defined crimes of hate when the victims are targeted because of their sexual orientation. Sexual orientation is now a legal category no longer unspoken in Topeka.

So, it's not over in Topeka, Kansas. Those who fought this good fight are more experienced, better organized, in touch with more people, and more visible to everyone as a force to be reckoned with. And they have set an agenda to which others must react rather than waiting for anti-gay forces to make the next move.

They'll return again after a short breather, to fight the next battle, to take the next step. That's how most permanent progress takes place, not in a straight-line fashion but through zigs and zags.

In the recruitment video for the Christian Coalition, Pat Robertson tells his followers that: "It's the last one remaining in the room who wins." These Christianists know that their fight is a long one, and their hope is to wear down their opponents so their opponents will walk out and allow Coalition members to be the last ones standing.

And the Christian Coalition did not reach the highpoint of its influence in a mere few years. They began their mailing lists in the 1964 presidential campaign of Barry Goldwater. Every defeat was a chance to add to their mailing list, refine their strategy, rewrite their language, and redefine their intentions.

Progressive leaders reach their goals because they stay in the room, especially in all the towns and cities in our country that Topeka, Kansas represents. They know it's a long battle. They get very tired, but they come back again and again.

Each time, the door of the closet opens a little further before it slams back shut again. With each effort it never closes as tightly as before.

It's happening everywhere, slowly, but surely. And it's because people like those in Topeka, Kansas, are making it happen against seemingly insurmountable odds.

On this Thanksgiving, thank you Topeka, Boise, Tulsa, Des Moines, Springfield, Birmingham, Albuquerque, Columbia, and Salt Lake City — from all of us. Thank you to the activists in small towns we never hear about, all the towns and cities hardly considered, even abandoned, by outsiders.

Remember what an old Rabbi said, "If you have a dream that can be fulfilled in one lifetime, it's too small."

Why Would Anyone Listen to Dr. Laura?

Popular, radio personality Laura Schlessinger has no psychological credentials. Her doctorate is in physiology. Her doctoral research studied fat deposits in rat testicles. A real psychologist like Harriet Lerner says, "I disagree with her on everything."

She doesn't listen to her callers fully and at length but cuts them off to push her agenda. She is full of moralistic advice and presents it in a curt, judgmental fashion that makes one wonder what unhealed psychological issues she is acting out on her callers.

Yet people call in and take the abuse she doles out to them. These callers sound like people who had been previously abused by life, who can't afford legitimate therapy, who have no sense of personal boundaries when it comes to their emotional issues, and who need more attention, particularly negative attention, from someone whose own psychological problems propel her to be their blaming and shaming mother. They would make great guests on "The Jerry Springer Show."

I have only heard portions of her show a few times when there seemed to be nothing else on radio as I drove across those distances that make rural America or as I rode with others who listened because they for some reason were soothed by her message of personal "responsibility." That message only slightly disguised the fact that she shamed a caller. I can't imagine that any of this would work on her upcoming TV talk show.

Her statements about LGBT people (homosexuality is a biological error" and homosexuals are "deviants") are indefensible. Her promotion of the negative and unsubstantiated stereotypes heard from religious and political extremists ("a huge portion of the male homosexual populace is predatory on young boys") is mean, incendiary, and abusive. Her calls for "reparative therapy" to convert people to heterosexuality are far out of touch with all mainstream psychological and counseling organizations.

And her denial in a February *San Francisco Examiner* interview that she has ever made "an anti-gay commentary" is a brash attempt to secure the appearance of her new TV program against growing criticism from LGBT organizations and their allies.

Dr. Laura is just one of the abusive talk show hosts that AM radio has produced since "the Fairness Doctrine" was scrapped by Congress. We could name others, but, as media analysts have pointed out, they have in common the promotion of a white, straight male agenda which defends the subordination of people to the white, heterosexual male who feels "embattled."

Though she is taking advantage of all the gains feminism has made for women, she calls us back to the "olden days" as much as Rush, G. Gordon, Don, and others are doing. She belongs with these men. They surely admire her, and her callers, men and women, must think this is the answer to their problems too.

To stop this abuse, a number of organizations have called for pressure on the Paramount Television Group to discourage her TV show's birth. Previous attempts by the Gay and Lesbian Alliance Against Defamation to work with Dr. L. have failed. Their next step is urging that every means of pressuring her business-minded producers and sponsors be applied to them.

At this point those in the LGBT community who object to such protests and pressure arise. They argue that such tactics infringe upon her first amendment right to free speech and that they constitute "censorship."

These detractors appear high-minded as they counsel people not to make their political and financial clout felt. They appear to take the high road in all of this rather than the path of direct action. And they sit on the sidelines and take pot shots at those who are doing something.

Meanwhile the mainstream media turns the story into how divided we are, just as it loves to do with any victimized group. So the headline of a recent Knight Ridder feature is: "Gays and lesbians divided over trying to silence Dr. Laura's TV show."

But this is not an issue of free speech. No one is saying that the abusive "Doc" can't express her viewpoints as freely as the rest of us. She can get up on the same human soap box as any of us.

No, this is an issue of crass, capitalist market strategy. Dr. Laura's speech is not free like yours or mine; it is bought and paid for. She has her expensive, nationwide, influential soap box because she makes money for sponsors who pay for it. She and her sponsors aren't concerned with free speech except to sound selflessly high-minded in defence of their interests when they feel attacked.

When will we wake up and realize that we are not dealing with equality of opportunity but the financial inequalities promoted by the American economy? And such capitalism has no morality. No one has ever been able to argue convincingly that the free market encourages moral decision-making. In fact, one station manager said to me in a television debate that he enjoyed the publicity. He was admitting, I responded that bigotry is acceptable for him if it's good for business.

The protests and pressure from potential listeners are exactly the strategy that will end Dr. L's bought and paid for speech and make it free again and equal to that the rest of us are supposed to have. At times even LGBT people have it because they fought for it.

Healing requires two activities. It means both that we heal from the effects of our past hurts and that we stop what is hurting us.

There is no excuse for Dr. Laura. Silence promotes her abuse of LGBT people as well as others whom our culture has already abused economically and emotionally.

But let's not turn this issue on ourselves and act like the poor old "Doc" is about to lose her first amendment rights.

Meeting a Friend While Progressives Fight Each Other

I met Gloria Nieto, Executive Director of the Santa Fe-based People of Color AIDS Foundation, in Atlanta in mid-November. Immediately she struck me as a compassionate, thoughtful, powerful, and winsome person that I'd like to know. She looked vaguely familiar too. That was because she had been a delegate from New Mexico to the Democratic National Convention and had spoken from the platform.

We were both attending the annual "Creating Change" Conference of the National Gay and Lesbian Task Force and had just responded from the floor to a panel convened to analyze the meaning of the 2000 presidential election. It turned out to be a panel of Democrats since a Green Party representative was never invited even though they were the only political party that had a booth at the conference, and Rich Tafel of the Log Cabin Republicans was a no-show. Apparently he hadn't notified the moderator that he had backed out.

Among the panelists' discussions of their preferences for a Gore presidency and the hope that a Bush presidency would be weak, was a disdain for Ralph Nader and the Greens.

When one young woman in the audience asked the panel to reflect about why there were no more than two young people at a session attended by about seventy people, the panelists' response blamed young people for lack of interest in such important things. And when a young man tried to explain that young queers felt disenfranchised from both dominant parties, he was silenced as one of those duped Nader supporters. The panel and most of the audience who silenced him didn't seem to see any connection between their two responses that put down the young people who had attended.

After the panel, an older, gay, white male told me that a vote for Nader was "criminal" and another that: "People who voted for Nader should be shot!" (I'm not making this up!) In all the talk about coalition building, the panel seemed to have no clue that this kind of attitude would only divide progressives further. The right wing should love that. They were playing into the hands of the Right.

Yet this is what we've done in this election. Progressives who voted Green took a long-term look at the Democratic Party, its corporate-funded stance, and its move toward conservatism under the dominance of the Democratic Leadership Council, and gave up. They may have been cheered by the populist language of Gore's acceptance speech, but they heard Joseph Lieberman reassure business executives in late August that Gore's populist talk should only be seen as "rhetorical flourishes."

In the final days of the race, we had already seen that Democrats could not believe that their party itself and its candidates had run a poor campaign. They could never have been responsible. So they turned on the Greens with more anger than they had ever expressed for Republicans. Filmmaker Michael Moore observed that "for the first time in years, [liberals] have finally found something to get angry about."

"It couldn't be the stands we have taken that lost us the election," defenders of the Democrat's anti-Green strategy said. "We surely aren't responsible for the outcome of this election. We are the victims of Ralph Nader." Not only were list-serves full of this discussion but famous liberals, including some national LGBT celebrities, were trotted out to warn, scold, shame, blame, and impress progressives to "get real."

Now, the arguments from both sides have been rehearsed over and over. Nader may not have been the best of the Greens to run for president, but I could think of better Democrats and Republicans than Gore and Bush.

There may have been strategic reasons to vote for Gore even against one's conscience. By election night everything had been said that could be said.

What was clear to me was that there were sincere people on both sides, many questioning the sincerity of the other side. And we saw liberals eating their own, acting out an important element of the victim role that non-dominant groups are conditioned to live. The media loved the divisiveness — now there was a reason for them to cover Ralph Nader.

So, after the panel, Gloria and I were being interviewed for national radio to present "opposing" sides of the Democrat/Green debate. The problem was that neither one of us bought into the victim role stuff.

We didn't even feel we were opposed to each other. Instead, I, a registered Democrat, lamented the fact that, rather than reaching out to the progressives whom the Democratic Party was losing, the public persona of the Party became one of blame and shame. That would surely widen the rift between liberals and progressives who need to work together, I emphasized.

Gloria spoke of her sympathetic understanding of the position of those who supported the Greens. She spoke also of her family and the need to see current programs maintained for them even though she could appreciate long-term Green ideals.

I could understand that. My own mother lives on Social Security, Medicare, and a meager pension fought for and secured by unions.

We were two activists torn between ideals and political realties, but not torn apart. And we could see that we had shared goals and wanted to work together. That was our common bond.

We blamed no one for the election's close outcome. We believed the best of each other. And we understood what columnist Molly Ivins meant when she recommended: "Where you can, vote with your heart. Where you must, vote with your head."

After that, when we ran into each other again and again at the conference, we not only had things to talk about, but I felt I was getting to know a friend I would never forget. In the midst of the shaming and blaming, the lack of asking what we can do to heal this open and widening rift in our community or, at least, not to make it worse, this was a bright spot. And I appreciated more and more that Gloria was at work for all of us.

A Leader's Resolution to Leave the "Victim Role"

I'm not sure where the idea of New Year's resolutions began, but I do know it produces a lot of feelings of guilt and failure. If they haven't been given up *for* Lent, resolutions are often given up *by* then.

Resolutions are decisions, decisions which indicate our good intentions, decisions which have to be remade regularly. We owe them to no one but ourselves, and being gentle and forgiving with ourselves this year is a healthy resolution to start with.

As members of one of the groups in a fear-based society that have been victimized by a dominant group, we may not have noticed that we are also conditioned by the institutions of our society to take the *role* of a victim. LGBT people are taught to live their lives in response to and in reaction to the dominant group, that the dominant group is "normal," and that not only our survival but our value depends upon the will of that dominant group. We even are taught to "eat our own" because we know what happens if we eat "them."

This is not to deny that there is actual victimization of LGBT people. That's obvious.

But resolving not to live the role we are supposed to live, creates a new personal stance to all of life that enables us to deal effectively, proportionately, and safely with the very real discrimination and oppression that is actually happening in the present moment. The result will have a profound effect on ourselves personally and on the communities with which we identify. We will all benefit.

Since each human relationship involves negotiation for how such roles are lived, those who have been victimized can end the victim role by making decisions that take their power back. We step out of our given role to find our real inborn selves.

And the very act of deciding not to live in the victim role is itself the first step out of it. Since these acts are decisions for oneself — not promises to anyone else — which reverse what has been learned from childhood, we will need to face any fears that would keep us from living on the basis of these decisions.

What might be some resolutions this new year for us and for how we relate to each other in a community which has been victimized as we refuse to live the victim role? If we take them on we'll slip. So, remember, we'll need to remake them monthly, weekly, even daily.

1. I decide that from this moment on I will never again live as a victim — live on the basis of lack of attention from others, of other people's evaluation of me, or by waiting for others to do what needs to be done, or expecting to be paid back for the love and attention and activism I express to others.

2. I will not live on the assumption that I will again be victimized.

3. I will stop complaining and obsessing about and rehearsing the patterns of "the right wing" and instead will plan a strategy of action to end what is hurting me personally.

4. I will treat each person who identifies with a group that treats me in a homophobic, heterosexist manner as a human being who stands before me in the present, not as a stereotype of "that group."

5. I will refuse to be abused by anyone and will therefore take charge of my own space and safety.

6. I will create safe spaces for all people to be, and I will explore the variety of meanings of being a gay man, lesbian, bisexual or transgender person.

7. I will not wait around for straight people to like me or for them to "get it right."

8. I will take the lead, organize, and set the agenda for myself and the movements with which I identify, not merely react to others and what they are doing.

9. I will not be afraid to make mistakes, or afraid that I will not "do it" eloquently or perfectly enough. And I will clean up, not deny, the messes I make in the process. Healing is messy. As we learned in kindergarten: "If you make a mess, clean it up."

10. I will seek to heal all the rifts among members of the my victimized community: gay men with lesbians; gay men and lesbians with bisexual people; gay men, lesbians and bisexual people with transgender people; young with old; old with young; "middle class" with working class LGBT people; white people with people of color; and leaders with leaders.

11. I will assume the best of those of us who have the courage to do something, no matter what I hear, until *I personally* talk to them and listen carefully to them *personally.*

12. I will never again live on the basis that anything negative that I believe about me has anything to do with my sexual orientation. I will never again blame and shame myself or anyone else for any reason.

13. I will set up a community of people around me who will not need to fix me but be committed to loving me unconditionally, listening to me carefully, and helping me express how I am feeling safely and in safety.

What a new year this could be with resolutions like these, no matter how often we might have to say "Oops," and remake them.

Politics

The Minor Details

It's Always Political and Far from Over

So you thought the courts would keep us safe and "the rule of law" and the Bill of Rights guaranteed our security, right? If last month's Supreme Court decision to hand the presidency over to the Republican candidate didn't open our eyes, nothing will.

It looks like Justice Scalia got his wish (expressed to confidants back in March) for a Republican president who might appoint him to the post of Chief Justice. The press reported that he threatened to resign from the Court if the country elected a Democratic president. Since he acted much like Bush's attorney through it all, let's hope he also secured nice end-of-the-year bonus checks for his two sons, who are partners in law firms representing George W.

Justice O'Conner now can retire to Arizona. At a party not long ago, her friends (and, oops, a reporter), heard her desire for a Republican win so that it would be safe for her to step down.

And I think Justice Thomas' wife should get some extra perks since now she can continue to submit resumes for the Bush II White House at the American Heritage Foundation.

What we've seen with remarkable clarity is what history has shown us happens in our courts through the "Dred Scott" decision and many less infamous Supreme Court decisions. Law is closer to politics than it is to finding the truth, and "justice" is seldom blind. As LGBT people, we are fortunate that the right combination of political appointments on the Supreme Court and an atmosphere of public activism in 1996 led to rejection of Colorado's anti-gay Amendment Two, approved by voters in 1992.

While some of us are celebrating gay arrival in shows like "Will and Grace" and "Queer as Folk," reality grinds on with the success, or uncomfortably close losses, of measures and initiatives designed to limit the rights of LGBT people. A wicked anti-gay measure in Nebraska to amend its constitution won overwhelmingly. A Maine measure to protect LGBT people from discrimination was defeated narrowly. A Nevada initiative against gay marriage passed easily. In Oregon, a measure that would deny funds to schools that taught that homosexuality was okay was just barely defeated. And in Vermont, anti-same-sex-union-Republicans overturned the Democratic majority in the House of Representatives, while the Governor who signed the bill only won after a tough campaign centering on the issue.

Richard Goldstein, executive editor of *The Village Voice*, writes that a backlash is taking place which is much like that of the 1920's when the pop culture of the Jazz Age hardened conservative resolve against the "loosening" of social mores, and in the 1960's when Richard Nixon won by scolding the counter-culture.

"Something similar is happening with the new acceptance of gays on television," he writes. "The more they are portrayed on screen as understandable human beings, the more threatening they seem off-screen." In addition, he argues, the very positive portrayal in mainstream media of those who have been mis-treated in the past also "blunts the reality of oppression."

Yet, this is happening at a time when LGBT people are com-ing to believe that activism is no longer necessary. We're on TV, so we must have made it. We have made some progress, so there's no need to fight. Everybody loves us, so we don't need to celebrate pride in who we are anymore. We're so accepted that we are living in a period that some of us are calling "post-gay."

How quickly we forget the lessons of history that the Supreme Court decision in Bush vs. Gore should make clear again. It's the politics of the situation that moves the courts, elects the judges, changes the laws, makes discrimination less and less profitable, and eventually even helps change hearts. It's the pressure we put on people and the constant presence we show to society, that keeps the human rights agenda from reversal.

And that means we cannot give up, lay down, or think that we have no more to do except marry, raise children, spend money, and mow our lawns. When all the others think the fight is over, those who remain to agitate for what they want, will secure it. And they must continue on in order to keep it.

Historian Howard Zinn in an essay entitled "Free Speech: Second Thoughts on the First Amendment" documents the history of U.S. courts' denial of first amendment rights. Though we might not want to face this, U.S. history shows that "to depend on the simple existence of the First Amendment to guarantee our freedom of expression is a serious mistake, one that can cost us not only our liberties but, under certain circumstances, our lives." (*Declarations of Independence*, 1990)

We have come a long way, and there will be a time when people who are "queer" will be accepted. But if the issues we want addressed and settled, such as simple equality and full legal acceptance, are important to us, we have quite a way to go.

Some of us may be able to afford to live above the fray to remove ourselves temporarily from the discrimination and prejudice. Our compulsion to spend is a compulsion to feel safe.

Some of us may blame other groups for our lack of progress. There are, after all, gay Neo-Nazis with web sites and chat rooms.

The Supreme Court has again reminded us that we are far from finished, and that we must think of things politically. Feminist activists are right: "The personal is political."

And this is the politics not of those leaders out there but the politics of the grassroots. Former Speaker of the House Tip O'Neil, reminded us that: "All politics is local." It's not limited to the politics of political parties. The politics that changes things consists of actions that relentlessly, proudly, and with bold and public openness, still continues to say, "We're here. And we're not leaving until we never have to leave."

Domesticating King and Co-opting Us

We just tripped over August 28, the 39th anniversary of Rev. Martin Luther King Jr.'s "I Have a Dream" speech. That speech, delivered in the shadow of the Lincoln Memorial to the 1963 March on Washington, has become his most popular.

It's inspiring, passionate, prophetic, and hopeful. It's his most recited speech, while others are ignored. And our culture has made it useful and loves to use it. By removing it from the context of King's total life and thought, we have woven it into a pattern we use to inhibit real, structural change.

We've popularized certain lines and images so that King doesn't really threaten the system. King can appear to place the entire blame for racial problems on individuals. Then, we preach that you, the individual, should just stop being prejudiced. Just say no!

It's only the fault of individuals, we can conclude. It has nothing to do with the way the institutions of our culture are conceived, setup, run, and financed, or what they teach, and how they make their profits. It has nothing to do with the dominant military-industrial-prison-media-corporate complex that finds itself in the middle of a major corporate crime wave today, denies that it's at fault, blames "a few bad apples," and works to re-hide it's sickness from sight.

But King knew better. He knew that there were entrenched structural problems with our way of doing things that required deep-rooted change.

The FBI and other "authorities" didn't target him because he told people they shouldn't be prejudiced. King didn't protest the Vietnam War merely because it reflected the white racism of individuals who promoted it. And King wasn't assassinated because he thought individuals alone needed to change.

In fact, King was assassinated while in Memphis to support better pay and conditions for its garbage workers. His life and work had become a challenge to the socio-economic system itself. He could see that our institutional structures embodied the deeper problem, and that they needed to change.

Protecting the structures is our cultural pattern. It's a pattern that explains how we try to fix things.

We reenact methods which we learned from our authoritative disciplinarian fathers. We blame individuals. Make people feel guilty, scared, ashamed, deviant, or sick. Tell them human nature is bad, or defective or essentially wild, greedy, selfish, sinful, or flawed. Pass more laws. Punish them more severely. Announce that we're "tough on crime." Threaten them with hell fire. Preach individual responsibility more. Find people to doctor statistics so it appears that these methods are successful — like the popular corporate business technique of inflating profits.

And when these old and tired methods still don't work, we do more of them — more laws, more prisons, stiffer punishments, more executions, more wars, more, more, more. In fact, if incarcerations continue to grow at the current rate in the U.S., it looks as if half of our population could be in prison by 2023. Now, that'll fix things!

Corporate problems with telling the truth? Punish some token executives.

Poverty? Call them lazy.

Cancer? Never suggest it's from companies polluting our environment but make money on the drugs these companies make for victims instead.

Teenage pregnancy? Scare them and deny them complete information.

Violent crime? Get everyone armed.

A lack of journalism that investigates institutions? Emphasize tabloid journalism and personal stories.

Problems with government leaders being bought? Scapegoat a few while both parties take money from the same sources.

Loss of jobs? Blame affirmative action or foreigners.

A growing economic disparity between the few rich and the many? Blame the many for being untalented, without ambition, lazy, and unwilling to take risks.

Drug use? Throw them all in prison.

But never get down to the societal conditions that might require radical change. And marginalize, demonize, and eliminate from the discussion anyone, no matter how good their supporting research is, that points to societal conditions that produce our problems. Never threaten the system. Let the institutions that produce wealth for the few and subsistence for the many grind on without change.

And what LGBT people have to face head on is that this is the system that blames us for the prejudice, discrimination, hatred, violence, sickness, and death we face. It wants to tell us that we are the problem and it wants us to believe that it's something about us that needs to change. The system doesn't want to change. It wants us to change.

It's a system that needs homophobia to sell its products but also wants our money. It intends to keep straight white males in charge but needs us to believe we can buy into its structures. It smiles at us when we look straight. It doesn't want our "lifestyle" to challenge its flawed ethics, its exploitation of normative heterosexuality, its limited definitions of humanity, or its priorities.

It's afraid that we'll rise up from some queer space and expect better for ourselves. So it loves to sell us alcohol and other addictions so that we don't feel that our lives are on the wrong track and decide that we need to change things to make our lives better, healthier, and deeply joyful. Let's face it, society around us doesn't experience a lot of that joy either.

It wants our AIDS organizations to act like straight-acting charities that settle for serving the afflicted and preach safe sex to individuals. It doesn't want them to question government and pharmaceutical company policies politically and economically. It prefers that they raise money from safe individuals and the private sector, like good little charities, and not take any dollars away from government priorities related to our war-based economic system.

Fear dominates our system as well as the corporate executives who seek more and more compensation on top of the current millions they receive because they fear our system's fragility. But our system and its leaders are really afraid that we'll change things, that our society may have to search for new answers, new definitions, and new ways to structure its institutions.

And change that makes a difference isn't easy. As one reviewer concluded his review of my book *Scared Straight*: "Although it would certainly be nice to invert the civilized world's thinking a little, it is also, quite frankly, just too much work."

The good news is that LGBT people and their allies can do it, and the reality is that we must. We need to take personal responsibility for our lives, sure. But the fact that we are often left outside the mainstream is not our fault. The system needs to, and can, change. To fit in is to betray ourselves and to deny the hope everyone needs.

And King knew that. As he said in words that are less famous: "The saving of our world from pending doom will come, not through the complacent adjustment of the conforming majority, but through the creative maladjustment of a nonconforming minority." (*Strength in Love*, 1963)

The Faithless Business of Funding "Faith Based Initiatives"

I t's pretty clear that an ultraconservative corporate executive agenda is beneath the Bush II administration's moves even more than it was in the Clinton administration. The Bush gang and his Congress are pursuing it with a vengeance.

Ending government social programs that could instead become money-makers in the hands of corporate executive friends is one of the administration's apparent central intentions in remaking government.

It's on track. Public health care, transportation, education, and social security programs have great potential for the kind of corporate executive profits pocketed by the top officials of Enron, Global Crossing, Tyson, WorldCom and the other corporations with "misreporting" problems.

The strategy for moving public non-profit programs into private apparently profit-making hands (meaning profits for executives) is to weaken or destroy those public programs. You can do this either through a constant, conservative-think-tank-created barrage of criticism, a combination of enforcing new requirements for a program while decreasing or denying adequate funding to the program itself, or both.

Merely adding further requirements to the public sphere (while, not coincidently, removing regulations from the corporate sector), such as mandatory achievement testing, without providing the additional funding needed to prepare for and administer the exams, is one example. Until they started doing so themselves, conservatives criticized so-called liberals for this, calling it "unfunded mandates."

Privatization is usually justified by the assumed common wisdom that the private sector can do anything more efficiently than government. The actual evidence that this is so, however, is seldom examined. The assumption that government should be run like a business seems to ignore the fact that the popular, long-running Dilbert comic strip is based on tons of ideas from people in business, not government. And its creator, Scott Adams, said he still has four more years of ideas from business that have been submitted to him.

One example of this assumed "success" in the area of education is Edison Schools, Inc., the nation's largest for-profit manager of public schools. Edison became a hit on NASDAQ with its shares trading at one time for as high as $38. But by 2002, Edison became another example, according to SEC investigators, of a company that misreported revenues and lacks an adequate system of accounting controls. By late 2002, its shares were selling for under a dollar. In Philadelphia it sold off textbooks and other supplies to pay its bills.

This privatizing model is behind the administration's funding of "faith-based initiatives." Again it's justified by the claim that religious organizations can do anything more efficiently than governments. And again, they cite no studies to prove this.

We know religious institutions pay their employees poorly in comparison to governments. They even rely on free volunteer labor. We know religious institutions can discriminate in employment of, and services to, LGBT people. We know top religious executives aren't volunteers but often well-paid bureaucrats with housing allowances and other perks such as not having to pay payroll taxes.

We know religious organizations are full of similar scandals and cover-ups as those that afflict big business. We know they have a privileged status that doesn't have to pay the property, real estate, sales, and other taxes other businesses do. We know they aren't required to publicly report what's really going on with their accounting.

But we don't hear of data that says these institutions are more efficient than governments. And without full reporting, how can we know?

We're just supposed to *believe* what religious leaders and their political supporters preach. That's where the faith is in government funding of "faith-based initiatives." They're no longer expressions of faith by the churches and their supporters themselves.

First, it used to be accepted that faith is to be active in good works. (C.S. Lewis once complained that Christians talk about doing good works but seldom about doing good work.) That has meant that faithful people give or tithe so that there is some sort of sacrifice of their wealth. It was the proof that God was more important to them than their money.

"Faith-based initiatives" however, allow religious people to spend tax money, *other peoples' money, yours and mine.* That means they can save more of their own money to build bigger estates and to feather their own nests. Their good works, then, become really our good works. How's that for faithlessness?

Second, faith-based people used to believe that there was some good, righteous, powerful, higher power who would see to it that the truth would win out. This God wasn't dependent upon kings, emperors, or governments for success.

"Faith-based initiatives" make government the guarantor of the success of their religion. They no longer trust in God or the Spirit to make things work – government will. How's that for faithlessness?

Third, faithful people used to believe that it was their job to send out missionaries, and even to be missionaries themselves. If they were full-time religious professionals, they'd even have to raise their own funds from other faithful to do so.

Not any more. Taxpayer funded "faith-based initiatives" bring in the non-believers who have needs that draw people to the initiative. The hardest part of evangelism is now the work of government funding. Religious people don't have to work as hard to "bring them in" to hear their message of salvation, or pay as much for it. How's that for faithlessness?

Isn't it obvious? What government funded "faith-based initiatives" make clear is that those who push them have very little faith in their God, in themselves, or in the power of their own good works. They also demonstrate that they just don't want to make the financial sacrifice that good works were supposed to take. In other words, we're the ones that are supposed to just believe, while they've given up the real proofs that they have any faith at all.

The First Independence Day of "United We Stand"

I t's the first of (we're assured) many Independence Days during The War on Terrorism. And LGBT people are expected
to be into "United We Stand" with the rest of our leaders
because the U.S.A. is better than other places — we have
human rights here we wouldn't have elsewhere, right? — and
because those terrorists who hate us might attack us again,
from anywhere at any moment.

Since the tragic and unjustifiable events of September 11,
2001, "the War" has become the dominant factor in American
politics. And it has developed into the perfect war for our system. It provides the solution for a nation whose economy since
the middle of the last century has been built on the need for
war to keep its industries booming, the stock market happy,
and its working people employed.

In the process, the Pentagon budget has become a money-
laundering scheme for military contractors. The Defense
Department's own audits indicate that one quarter of its budget
is unaccounted for. We've become accustomed to the Pentagon
buying over-priced hammers and widgets, to their willingness
to spend billions on unneeded and faulty weapons, and, no
matter how much a President has requested, to the Congress
consistently raising his request.

And it's bipartisan. It doesn't matter which party is in office.
Military contractors are thriving, their CEO's are receiving millions in compensation, their workers feel lucky just to have jobs,
and the public is willing to send more of its increasingly more
hard-earned tax money to these corporations at the expense
of human social programs.

We've learned from the administration that this war will
never end (How good a guarantee is that for the security of
future military-industrial complex profits!), that the enemy can

lurk anywhere — even in our midst, and that the enemy is just plain inhuman, a part of a full-fledged "Axis" of evil.

We've been told that the war on drugs, another endless war and one that we've been losing badly, is really a part of this bigger war. We've been told that we may have to fight this war anywhere in the world and seem to be poised to attack in Iran and Columbia.

All that accompanies this "War" — fear of imminent danger (prepare again to "duck and cover"); the quaking of the "loyal opposition" party in fear that they won't appear loyal enough; the marginalizing, dismissing, and pathologizing of peace groups; the dominance of the military-industrial complex in domestic decision-making; the centrality of the "intelligence" community; government monitoring of dissidents; the limiting of civil liberties for "security reasons" — has the marks of the old Cold War. That's not surprising since our current administration's leaders learned to understand reality only in Cold War terms.

One difference today is that the development of high-tech weapons has ensured us that there will be fewer of our own military (the side of goodness) coming back in body bags. Another is that the American media are dominated by fewer corporate media owners, and these few are even more invested in the success of the administration and its sponsors than ever before. So, they self-censor and act as cheerleaders more than they are public-spirited critics. Still another is the media's attempt to make an unelected, communicationally-challenged "president" look legitimate with stories that try to convince us that he's not as slow as he appears to be. He really, really does, they gush, represent true leadership.

The most important difference is that we are now the only superpower. We're in charge of it all. We're the only game on the block. We're number one. We can bully anyone into what we want. We have the power and might.

Never known for the subtly of his thinking, as the "President" says: "If you're not for us, you're against us." And you can be sure we'll straighten out any country that doesn't agree with us.

No wonder the Dutch Parliament is outraged over the "American Service Members Protection Act" just passed by a bipartisan vote in the U.S. Congress. It authorizes our "President" to use "all means necessary" to free any American held by the International Criminal Court in The Hague. So the "President" now has congressional authority to invade the Netherlands, even using atomic weapons if he wants. The Dutch have dubbed it "The Hague Invasion Act." So, to quote another Western: "Just do what we say and you won't get hurt."

We LGBT people are supposed to support this because we're all united. We're all in this together. Our leaders should be trusted to do the best and we've got to recover our security and get revenge on anyone who would make us feel insecure.

In the meantime, the regimes we support in the Near East treat LGBT people as useful tools for their purposes while U.S. leaders say nothing in protest. Egypt is pressing prosecutions of gay men. The American-backed Saudi dictatorship has increased its brutal executions of gay men in order to protect its position from right-wing Muslims by proving the Saudi family consists of really good, orthodox Muslims after all. To do that, gay men are disposable. Still, "United We Stand," right?

And back here at home, how are LGBT people treated for buying into this national unity? Well, in bipartisan fashion, three Democrats and three Republicans from the House of Representatives couldn't wait another minute for "the War's" end to introduce a constitutional amendment against us. It's the Federal Marriage Amendment that reads in part: "Marriage in the United States shall consist only of the union of a man and a women." And "United We Stand, Freedom for All," right?

I know it sounds queer to many people, but I'm choosing to stand united with Ohio congressman Dennis Kucinich, the head of the Congressional Progressive Caucus. A year ago this Democrat defied his John Ashcroft-confirming, corporate bought party leaders to introduce legislation to create a cabi net level agency dedicated to waging peace and the study and promotion of conditions that are conducive to peace.

I'd been so jaded by my U.S. war-is-inevitable up-bringing that I too rolled my eyes when I first heard of the idea. With most, I guess, I believed that the idea of peace is totally unrealistic. War will always be with us.

But then again, since I see no future in "The War" of United We Stand, I figure LGBT people have at least as much of a chance with the peace dissidents than with those who'll use us under some slogan of unity for this everlasting "war" and then portray us as threats to society to scare up voters. I'm standing united with the peace dissidents in hope for real freedom.

Weapons of Mass Distraction:
Duct Tape and Cover

I agree. We should definitely be on Orange Alert. None of the advances LGBT people have made is safe. Though we've made some headway, in the last few months we've also seen an upsurge in efforts to thwart progress and undo legal victories.

In addition to dozens of attempts to undo protections in cities, counties, and schools, for example, in early February Minnesota Republicans introduced a bill that would delete legal protections based on sexual orientation or gender identity. Never giving up, they're back again to attempt to undo one of our most liberal state's 1993 laws. A Colorado legislative committee killed a bill that would have granted legal recognition to same-sex couples. A Missouri measure would make it difficult for school systems to adopt policies protecting LGBT youth. And full Southern Baptist pressure is on Nashville to keep the city from protecting LGBT people.

In December, the U.S. Supreme Court took up a challenge to Texas' sodomy law. Among other states, Texas currently makes it a crime to engage in "deviate sexual intercourse" — oral and anal sex — with a person of the same sex.

Whether this Court's interest in examining the law is a good thing or not, we'll have to see. A slim majority may decide the case. But it will be outside societal pressure that will force their decision more than real questions of fairness, justice, equality, humanity, and compassion.

Remembering the very manner in which they chose a "president" should make us feel insecure when sodomy is in the hands of these justices. This Court is a highly political entity searching for judicial reasons to shore up its prejudices. We'd better keep up political pressure while we hope for their best.

So we need to be on high alert, alert for more attempts to undo what has been gained. And we can't assume that allies will automatically protect us. We've got to encourage them. Obsessed anti-gay bigots come back again and again and again. This is no time to settle down.

But the "president" and company — the "United We Standers" — know how to distract us while un-doing our rights and moving ahead on anything they've planned to do. With war, fear, and imminent terrorist attacks as weapons of mass distraction, their imperial-international and redistribution-of-wealth-national agenda can move forward under the radar.

And nothing they've done to distract the public has slowed their efforts to undo women's choice, to ensure advantages for rich white males, to shift the tax burden away from their upper-class friends, to subsidize churches (mostly right-wing ones), to eliminate any control on big business, and to re-define the U.S. as a military-economic "American Empire."

The march to war proceeds with every distraction in the book. Colin Powell appears to be the administration's most trusted spokesperson. So he gets the out-on-a-limb assignment of convincing U.S. citizenry that war for the American way is necessary and inevitable. But he'd better come up with more impressive information than he was fed for his February 5 speech to the UN Security Council.

Powell actually quoted a British intelligence report that, instead of being based on whatever "British intelligence" is supposed to do, plagiarized three previously printed papers, one a decade old research paper by a student at the Monterey (California) Institute of International Studies. Not only did Powell attempt to pawn this off as the fresh work of intelligence sources, but the British report didn't even bother to correct the typographical and grammatical errors in the original student paper.

France, Germany, and Belgium, NATO allies least dependent on U.S. economic and political coercion for their survival, balked at the administration's distractive strategies. They want real evidence, while our administration tries to bully, shame, and marginalize dissenting nations as weak, effeminate, stupid, even quite queer. U.S. administrations have never had much use for Europe anyway, unless, like the current British government, they saddle up to ride along with us.

They've pictured Europeans as less manly than us rugged, frontier, shoot-first-ask-questions-later, cowboy, hyper-masculine Americans. After all, Europeans can't really be manly. We always have to save them militarily. And look how they seem to accept so many queer things. Look how the European Union is moving to fully accept LGBT people, even in the military. That's not real red-blooded American manhood.

How much less does our administration value the February third vote of the African Union, representing 53 nations, that declared its opposition to the U.S. unilateral pro-war position? This, of course, seems to have been mostly ignored by our corporate, war-dominated, white-faced media.

And how long has it taken our media to recognize what U.S. historians like Howard Zinn are calling the largest anti-war movement in U.S. history? They've tried to downplay it. They continue to underestimate its numbers even though it's one of the few war protest movements that has gathered such steam before a war has begun. And how often have we seen "the left" on debate shows like CNN's Crossfire represented by a "from the left" host who's anti-war?

There's much that this war is supposed to distract us from. We're not supposed to care about the largest budget deficit in history – even without adding in the up-coming additional appropriations to pay for the war itself. We're not supposed to care about the curtailing of our freedoms in the bipartisan "USA Patriot Act" and its proposed expansion. We're not supposed to complain when our states struggle to cut social services and throw more of the already poor into shelters and food lines.

And we're not supposed to care that building that unchallenged American empire, a goal of the new U.S. foreign policy in this administration, is how we're being known throughout the real world. We're not supposed to believe that defeating Iraq and replacing it with a "friendly" regime has anything to do with taking control of the world's second-largest, most-valued oil fields. Or that a U.S. general running Iraq will mean a U.S. vote on oil-prices in OPEC. Even the Iraqi opposition to Saddam Hussein, which welcomed U.S. military pressure, is now beginning to realize that they won't be in charge when it's over, unless they kowtow to U.S. demands.

And it's certainly a way to include LGBT people in the distractions while the same people at the center of doing so are planning new measures to make sure we are excluded from the reality of U.S. life.

I was watching a CNN reporter compare the current official advice to stock up on duct tape, plastic sheeting, dried food, and water so we're prepared for inevitable terrorist gas, chemical, and nuclear attacks. After replaying the old Cold War "duck and cover" films, she noted that our government knew then that ducking under a blanket or school desk after "you see a bright light" would do nothing to save us. But, she said, that was okay because: "It made people feel better. We felt as if there was something we could do." And she said it with a very straight face!

We're being distracted by something that will accomplish nothing for us. We're being told there's something that we can do that will save us, while what will really save us is very different and has nothing to do with Iraq. We are really being threatened with losing our rights, as humans and as LGBT people. And we're forgetting what American investigative journalist I. F. Stone declared was the first rule of journalism: "All governments lie."

The Pitiful State of Gay Politics

About 38% of the registered voters went to the polls across the U.S. last month. Many chose on the basis of what a lot of non-voters feel: Democrats have little to offer that Republicans aren't already doing.

This time, unlike the 2000 presidential election, Democrats can't use the Green Party as their scapegoat for another uninspiring, weak-kneed campaign. They have to take the responsibility themselves.

Let's face it. The Republicans have set the tone for successful campaigns today, and it's not nice. So being nice doesn't win any more. Democrats will have to stand for something and act as if they are willing to put everything on the line for it. It would be as if they have principles and constituencies they're not willing to compromise.

The scary response from the outgoing Minority leader of the House was that to win more votes the Democrats need to become more mainstream. Of course, that means more conservative, more like Republicans. He wasn't alone either. It's the New Democratic "wisdom."

The choice of a Democratic House Minority leader who is a real alternative to Republicans offered hope. In the past, San Francisco Rep. Nancy Pelosi was actually unafraid of the label "Liberal." She broke from party leaders to vote against the Iraq war resolution. She openly supported same-sex marriage. She actually said that one of her goals is to make sure that people know the difference between the two major parties. Now that she's in the Democratic leadership, will she, like her predecessor Dick Gephardt, cave in order to be seen in the Rose Garden by the "President's" side?

In the midst of all this, LGBT politics are in a sorry state. When it comes to our national political climate, we're expected to settle for something that's far from proud. It's down right pitiful.

An increasing number of people claim that there's no difference between the two major political parties. But that's not true when it comes to LGBT issues. The difference is clear if not happy.

Republicans would rather have LGBT people go away. For them, LGBT people are a nuisance.

The radical right who dominate the Party do everything to make that happen. It's such an obsession that they can't let it go. And they know that the "moderates" (who used to be called conservatives) will cave in on LGBT rights to save their own skins. No one will sacrifice power, votes, or donations.

Even gay Republicans are unwilling to identify with the rights of LGBT people as a whole if they are well-off enough to be protected. At least that's what the leader of the group founded to represent our interests in the "Grand Old Party" wrote this past year.

Rich Tafel, Executive Director of the Log Cabin Republicans, argued that there is no need for the Congress to enact the Employment Non-Discrimination Act (ENDA), banning employment discrimination based on sexual orientation. While most LGBT people can't identify with Tafel's assurances, he asserts, along with very straight Republican leaders, that our corporations are already adding any needed protections. Who wants government regulation of corporate America? Regulations might require them to spend some money to protect us. Of course, most of these same Republicans who agree with Tafel *do* support "good" government regulations such as the Defense of Marriage Act (DOMA)."

So, in the midst of our corporate and white-collar crime wave, Tafel aligns himself with that corporate-run order and with those white, males who are high enough in the class structure to buy themselves out of the most overt discrimination. He's aligned with the politicians who would rather have us keep quiet. He's telling us we shouldn't make an issue of employment discrimination nor seek the support of our federal government.

In response to that Log Cabin endorsement of the conservative agenda, Republicans are pleased, some Democrats are "we told you so" aghast, and the Log Cabiners, like lap-dogs, continue to feel honored by the scraps of attention Republican leaders toss them.

So, the only alternative LGBT people are supposed to have is the Democratic Party. That's the party of "New Democrats" such as smiling, compromising Bill Clinton, whom the Democrats tell us "has done more for gay people than any former President."

It's clear that most Democratic politicians assure us that they're really on our side, especially when it comes to asking for our votes. They argue that Democrats aren't as bad as Republicans. And they scapegoat progressive critics of their party as it grows less able to inspire its traditional constituents, such as labor and working people. Progressive critics, they say, should be ashamed because they're "the reason the Republicans are successful."

There's no doubt that LGBT people are useful to Democratic politicians as long as the politicians' own votes, donations, and power aren't on the line. But, with few exceptions, Democrats don't want to lose their positions either. Their leaders may sincerely want to work for us, but (and we must accept this with an appreciative smile) they "have to compromise," you see. And by that they mean they have to compromise on our issues.

"We'd love to follow through, but you'll just have to wait." "We had to vote for DOMA for your own good in the long run." And remember, they keep telling us, it could be worse. So, where's the evidence that these Democratic "friends" will stand up for us if anything of theirs is threatened?

During this past campaign, a gay man hired to bring out the LGBT vote for a Democratic incumbent assumed that we should understand that the candidate could not be seen at gay functions for fear of losing the more rural vote. I guess we're like the relatives no one wants to be seen with.

The candidate lost anyway. Even compromising me and my rights didn't help.

That's what LGBT people are supposed to accept. And then, of course, we are fighting an ever-lasting "war against terrorism." So, even more we're supposed to put off all our interests. You'd think, then, they'd all wait to pick on us, since they expect us to support "United We Stand" and all that. But no. Liberals compromise us; conservatives of both parties never compromise.

Now the "it could be worse" argument works as long as the Democrats win with it. But it's getting clearer that the strategy isn't working that well.

So, our choices seem to be to go with the winners, the Republicans, who don't want us out and proud, or with two losers: the Democrats who will compromise us for their fading hopes of winning nationally, or the Greens who have same-sex marriages, equal rights, and anti-gay bias in the military written into their party platform.

The Greens are making some progress. There are now 70 elected Green public officials around the country. Though that's improving, it's still small. But at least when Greens lose, it's not with the strategy of refusing to stand up for us in order to stay in office.

What a sorry state LGBT politics is in today. And the two major parties argue that we should somehow proudly settle for this. We should settle for Republican dismissal and Democratic compromise. Well, that's just pitiful.

And They Say We're Sick?

There's a lot of talk now about how great American ideals are. But on this Independence Day I'm afraid they look more like these:

We value corporate executives if they keep stock prices up, not if they produce a product that enhances human life or if they spend corporate profits to maintain water and air that won't kill us.

Our politicians tell us, unlike those of most nations, that killing a killer is a way to teach that killing someone doesn't solve anything.

We execute a man who robs a convenience store and kills one clerk for $45 in order to buy food for his family. But tobacco executives who knew their product was deadly, advertised that it was safe, spiked cigarettes with further nicotine to make it even more addictive, targeted our teens, covered-up their crime, paid off our politicians, killed millions of people, and made billions of dollars, we let off if they promise not to advertise their product inappropriately. And we teach that that is justice.

We teach our boys that they can receive medals for killing other men but could be killed for loving other men, all in the name of American manhood.

We actually use words like "do-gooder," "liberal," "bleeding heart," "tolerant," "sensitive" and "welfare" as put-downs.

We use sex to sell our goods and services and we make people feel guilty if they ever should act sexually.

We use words like "virtue" (as in "she lost her virtue") and "immorality" (as in "nations fall when immorality becomes rampant") and we mean sex, not how we treat the needy among us or how we value our neighbors.

We're suspicious of anyone who is having too much fun. Pleasure should be put off till later.

We assume our "better" workers will be workaholics, as if workaholism isn't a fatal disease that destroys families, relationships, and individuals.

We allow half of the human beings in our country to make only 75% of what the other half makes for the same work just because they are female. We won't even pass an Equal Rights Amendment.

We teach our boys that the worst thing they can be is "a girl" — throw like a girl, run like a girl, talk like a girl — and that rubs off on the confidence of our girls too.

We teach our girls that, though they may try to do otherwise, their real value is in sacrificing their own dreams to please a man and live for their children. In fact, they should feel guilty if they don't.

We teach boys to be violent in sports and life in order to prove they're real men. Then we lock them up when they actually act it out, unless it makes money for a billionaire team owner.

We take people of different shades of pink-, peach-, and cream-colored skin and lump them together as "white" so that they don't fight among themselves and so they have privileges that people with darker skins don't have.

We've built, and we defend, an economy that needs war in order to keep it going. If we were not the major arms supplier to the world and our tax money didn't subsidize a giant weapons industry, our economy would collapse.

We value heroes who shoot over-sized guns like Rambo and Arnold, while we put down those who propose other ways to solve our problems.

We criticize workers when they do cooperate together in labor unions even though if they hadn't stood up against the guns of our police and military we wouldn't have an eight-hour workday, a five-day workweek, any workers' benefits, the idea of "overtime," or any control on employers' greed.

We're the only civilized nation in the world that does not value all human beings enough to guarantee adequate health care because our insurance companies wouldn't make such huge profits and we'd have to wait in line for tummy-tucks, face-lifts, and breast enhancements.

We have developed a national wage structure that promotes a lifestyle of dependency in richer people — they're dependent upon service personnel receiving low wages so the rich can live well. Yet we fear that "the poor" might become the ones "dependent" on others.

We blame undocumented aliens for problems created by Savings and Loan crashes, political paybacks, industry incompetence, and the failures of our corporate leaders to plan the future beyond their own stock options, while even our politicians hire them to do their yard work, baby-sitting, and house cleaning.

We have happily created and value an economic gap between the top and the bottom which out-paces any third world country.

We value newspapers with full sections devoted to sports ("It's just a game." Right!) and only one or two pages to understanding what's going on in the world.

We talk a good line about the value of education and how valuable our children are, but we pay teachers and anyone else who is responsible for our children so poorly that even our children get the message that we really value almost anything more than education.

We believe that we should pay attention to the moral preaching of an organization we've made our largest Protestant denomination, the Southern Baptist Convention, even though it was founded to promote slavery. And that gives them the right to scold us?

We hunt through the Bible, religion, and our traditions to find verses, pronouncements, and long-held attitudes in order to promote our current prejudices.

Now these are the values of a society that says that transgender and bisexual people and lesbians and gay men are sick and immoral just because LGBT people believe everyone should have the right to love anyone?

How did we ever start believing that?

Our country has so much possibility, but it is very, very sick. We can choose to buy into this sickness in order to fit in, or we can affirm our right to love, we can say the problem is not us, and we can change things. This society is crazy. LGBT people are just fine — unless they join in.

Society

The Minor Details

It's Time We Listened to Every Theory, No Matter How Crazy We Think It Is

About 15 years ago I walked into an LGBT bookstore in Denver. I remember that one of the pieces of free literature I picked up was an article reporting the results of scientific studies of the use of "poppers," the recreational name for amyl nitrate. The article indicated that there was growing evidence that its continual use suppressed the immune system.

That's the kind of information that I store away for future reference. I would have thought that it was common knowledge, but I don't think the scientific warning dampened its use in the gay male community to "enhance" sex. It's even used by the most educated among us.

I think the problem with such scientific studies is also one of their virtues. Scientists report their results in precise and nuanced form with phrases such as "It is likely," or "Evidence seems to show," or "There is a probability that," or "We find a possible correlation here." It's up to the rest of us to decide whether this scientific probability is enough to change our behavior or our thinking.

We can cling to scientific statements about what could probably happen and apply it to our life ("A high cholesterol diet has been shown likely to increase the chance of heart attacks.") or we can cling to the "fudge" words and do whatever we wanted to do anyway. The fact is, scientists seldom make absolute statements. And I'm used to that and expect it from them. It seems that that's good science.

That's not what I hear when I hear mainstream doctors and researchers discuss alternative theories to the causes of AIDS. What I hear is an attitude of condemnation, dogmatism, anger and demonizing. It's like listening to the medieval Church censor, condemn, and cast out it's heretics.

I'm not saying that the so-called AIDS dissidents are correct. But I don't believe that the public response of the AIDS establishment is helpful. A recent newsletter of one AIDS organization compared the message of the AIDS dissidents (called "AIDS denialists") with the claims of the tabloids that the moon landing was faked, that Elvis lives, and that Mars men have invaded the earth. Such sensationalist comparisons will be appreciated only by the already convinced. Those who aren't will experience them as distancing.

Of course, the argument of mainstream HIV-AIDS advocates for using such a divisive tactic is that lives depend on the truth as they see it. People might use the AIDS dissidents' arguments to give up their medicinal regimes.

But the argument of the AIDS dissidents is also that lives depend on the truth as *they* see it. Most people seem to argue this way about anything.

The AIDS establishment argues that the evidence is overwhelming and medications that they've developed have been effective. But the AIDS dissidents argue that we're not getting all the scientific facts, that people are living just as long without medication, that too much research money is available only for those who follow the party line in AIDS research, and that too much profit is being made by powerful pharmaceutical conglomerates off of the epidemic. Whereas there is little money to fund alternative research and non-medicinal solutions.

So here we are in the midst of an epidemic that spans the globe, an epidemic in which drug companies have become concerned about their profit margins and stock values while the poor of the world can't afford the drugs, an epidemic without a known vaccine, an epidemic with medications that are again beginning to fail us. And we are demeaning any possibilities for new avenues of investigation and demonizing the voices who are shouting for alternative paths.

One is reminded of the early days of ACT-UP. They were obnoxious, in-your-face, aggressive, and disorderly. They were trying to get a government to care about the dying, and a president to just use the word AIDS. They were demonized, and they paved the way, as such radicals do, for the establishment to listen to calmer voices and to change AIDS policy. That's what dissidents often do in American history. They scare the powers that be so that those powers listen to the moderates.

Most AIDS organizations today are anything but policy influences. They are afraid to offend their donors and their funding sources. They have settled for helping the afflicted and passing out condoms rather than affecting AIDS policy or challenging the corporate profits to be made off of the disease and its victims. They often are quite closeted when it comes to their LGBT administrators and clients.

What the AIDS dissidents are teaching us may be that there is more than drugs and condoms in this fight. It's time to talk about the lifestyle choices that compromise the immune system and may make HIV take in some and not others.

I'm not talking about laying another guilt trip on people about their sex lives. That doesn't work either.

I'm talking about some real quality of life issues. How do the overuse of antibiotics, the use of drugs, the high rate of alcohol abuse, poor and mal-nutrition, environmental pollution, and internalized homophobia help destroy an immune system and make it open to the syndrome of effects we call AIDS?

This is too great an epidemic to shut out any voices. We are not near its end. So we'd better not be acting like the establishment that cut out Galileo and other dissidents. We better listen to all voices, even the ones we think are the craziest.

I'm not saying we'll change our theories about HIV-AIDS though it wouldn't be the first time in human history that we've done so regarding disease. I'm just hoping that we'll listen carefully. We may find that we have complimentary ideas to reconcile and some bigger issues to tackle in order to end the epidemic.

In the meantime I am haunted by the words of a nineteenth century German philosopher, Arthur Schopenhauer: "Ever-truth passes through three stages before it is recognized. In the first it is ridiculed, in the second it is opposed, in the third it is accepted as self-evident."

Why We Should Be Standing Up for the Rights of Others

L GBT people often find it hard to understand why others who have suffered discrimination don't just get the point and stand up for the rights of sexual minorities. In some cases victims of racism, sexism, and classism even function as the point people for maintaining discrimination against LGBT people.

It was convenient for the predominantly white, right-wing Republicans who opposed adding sexual orientation to one city's anti-discrimination ordinance, to have an African American minister as the spokesperson for their cause. Didn't he see, I tried to explain to him, that those white people would never even invite him to their homes for dinner? Didn't he see that he was a member of a racial minority being used once again by white people? For him, instead, being against LGBT equality was more important than recognizing his usefulness to white conservatives.

Actually, though, it's understandable. Why would people who have fought against continual discrimination want to take on additionally the discrimination faced by LGBT people? And the fear that there aren't enough resources and attention to go around (an assumption basic to our Capitalism that gets applied to human relations) means that devoting resources and attention to ending LGBT discrimination might take both away from them and their own fight to end discrimination.

Any culture that can convince white, working class people to vote for — even argue for and bet their life on — political parties bent on favoring the economically upper ten-percent by making scapegoats of LGBT people, people of color, and women, has been effective at keeping all the suffering groups apart. Groups on the receiving end of discrimination get so caught up in fighting internally and with other victim groups that they aren't able to effectively change the larger institutions in which these discriminations are embedded.

And blaming Affirmative Action, the perceived gains of minorities and women, "liberal" policies, and other attempts to level the playing field for every human being, maintains a status quo that needs scapegoats while it continues to promote further economic disparity. If one were trying, one could hardly invent better strategies to prevent deep-rooted change.

Frankly, it's hard to get people to see that all of the discriminations go together and that freedom comes to everyone only when all inequality ends. Maybe we don't want to see this because the task seems too daunting. Maybe we don't want to face it because even we who have been in minorities might have to face our own fears and prejudices. Maybe we just don't want to admit that we have prejudices, even if they're obvious to many around us.

As members of one of those victimized groups, this means that we LGBT people must face the prejudice and discrimination that we carry individually and often maintain institutionally. And just as it does for others, this may feel very difficult when we're just trying to deal with what may be coming at us.

One of the things I've noticed though is that those of us who are able to live outside the most blatant examples of LGBT oppression — maybe because we have enough funds to buy our way out of it or, at least, to create a more well-appointed closet — are no less prejudiced. It's not the level of our victimization that seems to make the difference.

Certainly the gay slur has been used to keep minorities in their place. Calling the African American boy a "fag" or "queer" because he is uninterested in sports and would rather read, write, and study, has helped keep many brilliant men from contributing to changing racism. Using machismo to keep Hispanic boys in a hyper-masculinity has often kept them from being effective agents of change. And treating any women as weak, lacking power, and dependent has at times functioned to keep them from changing the multiple oppressions played out on women of color.

But, let's face it, LGBT people are filled with the prejudices of our culture as well. Notice how we buy into the stereotypes that keep some allies far from us. Thinking of Jews as all (or even mostly) rich and in control of world financial resources, is not only inaccurate but also anti-Semitic. Buying into any of the stereotypes of people of color, keeps potential allies at bay and promotes racism. Accepting the AM talk radio driven scapegoating of others for white male distress, is to promote the lifestyle of discrimination that ultimately comes down on us.

Believing without question mainstream media stories about other discriminated people, is to forget how media stories about our pride parades and the hate crimes directed against us are presented as sensationalized, distorted, or lacking in enough depth to explain what really happened and why. The triumph of TV "newsac" and the USA Today style newspaper with its abbreviated stories, splashy color, diversionary emphasis upon sports and business, and treatment of issues as personal problems not societal ones, is evidence of the victory of popular misunderstanding.

When white LGBT people don't listen carefully to, seek to understand, and believe the complaints of people of color, or when gay men do not listen carefully to, seek to understand, and believe the accusations and complaints of women, we are doing exactly what we hate when straight people do it to us.

Don't we dislike how straight people tell us we've not really been discriminated against and that what we call discrimination isn't really that? Don't we get angry when we are portrayed as whiners? Or when they say we're just too sensitive? Don't we hate it when straight people go into denial about their issues with us? And can't we see the similarities when we do the same things with others?

If we're going to expect understanding from the many others who have also been victims of our system of multiple discrimi-nations, it seems to me that we're going to have to be bette allies for them. We've got to be convinced that all oppressions are connected. We're going to have to face our part in this even if it's mostly been unintentional and unconscious.

It means we have to learn that we're a part of the problem when we maintain the societal structures that need to keep people apart so that we all don't rise up together and make it better for all of us. To start, we've got to see the connections our experiences of discrimination and hatred have with those of others.

Laramie Beyond the Media

I saw *The Laramie Project*. It refused to leave my mind long after the curtain came down. I realized what it did for me that most of the media, gay and straight, around Matthew Shepherd's death had not.

Since the play first opened in Denver in February 2000, performed by the Tectonic Theater Project, it has become a part of our national theatrical repertoire. I saw it as the opening production of the 28th season of the Unicorn Theater in Kansas City, Missouri, a venue where provocative, thoughtful, edgy works are the norm.

The Unicorn performed it with "that fence" reconstructed across the stage. You get the picture. Who could forget that image? But even if I knew all I wanted about the events surrounding Matthew Shepherd's brutal murder, *The Laramie Project* still took me further.

Four weeks after the murder, nine members of the Tectonic Theater Project visited Laramie, Wyoming to collect interviews from its residents. That became the material for the play. They returned to Laramie in November 2000 to perform it there. Reports indicated that those in attendance were moved as well.

Matthew Shepherd's fate became a national rallying point for "Hate Crime Laws" even where, as in Wyoming itself, they were never enacted. His parents became some of those national spokespersons who never asked for that status but who took up a cause that many would rather not face, much less discuss.

What struck me more and more as I thought about it was how this play took me beyond three of the images we'd been given about the events based upon how it was reported and analyzed— images which distort the truth to soothe mainstream America.

The first image was to portray Matthew Shepherd, the brutally tortured and murdered University of Wyoming student, as a "martyr."

There's little question that his death provoked some in this country to reconsider their attitudes toward the treatment of gay people. There is little question that it was the impetus for activism for some others. In that sense, we may be consoled by the idea that, "Good came out of evil."

But Matthew Shepherd was not a martyr. Martyrs choose to give up their lives for a cause. He didn't have a choice. His life wasn't given but taken, stolen from him, literally beaten out of him. He wasn't asked. And that's something we must never forget.

To call him a martyr, as both the gay and straight press did, is to cover up too quickly the fact of a life violently stolen. It was brutalized and ripped from him in the way life has been robbed from many LGBT people before and since. And that hasn't ended.

Judy Shepherd, his mother, knows. The truth to be shouted loudly is that he's not alone. This was not an isolated incident, media people. He's one of hundreds in the last decade, most of whom were quietly forgotten.

The many got no media attention. So, Matthew Shepherd is a symbol not of a life given up for a cause but of an on-going epidemic of violence against LGBT people, a reminder of all those whose lives were taken, most brutally. He shouldn't be used to make us feel better about it in any way. We've yet to finish mourning our legions of tortured dead.

The second image the media played upon was an attempt to make him the "boy next door." They wanted him to be wholesome," to look the part of the innocent kid, intelligent, with earning potential, and so "all-American." They wanted to believe that he was somehow not like others — that he didn't deserve" it because he didn't fit any stereotypes of LGBT people.

Now, he didn't deserve it. There's no question about that. But neither does any person deserve violence, murder, brutality, or any type of discrimination, no matter how they do or do not fit anyone's views of the "all-American boy."

And it didn't matter, though many seem to think it did, whether he had been interested in sex with his murderers. It didn't even matter whether he propositioned them. It didn't matter whether he turned down their propositions.

Yet the media portrayal, which reminds us of our culture's sickness around sexuality, says "all-American boys" wouldn't do those things.

Even if the "all-American" boy was (shudder to think of it) interested in sex, there's no justification for his murderers doing any more than responding: "No thank you. We're not interested." A man showing interest in another man should never be portrayed as filthy or criminal, but rather as giving a compliment.

The third image of the media's portrayal of the brutal murder of this gay young man, was to picture his killers as "not like us." That was important because it lets "mainstream Americans" off the hook.

They were "red necks," "low-life," of low intelligence, extreme right-wing fanatics, no-good, born to trouble, etc. You know the picture. They weren't like us "normal," regular, decent, middle class folk.

It was like believing that the only people who harbor any white racism are the Ku Klux Klan or the Neo-Nazis. We're clean, innocent, and in no way responsible. We're off the hook on that one too.

How convenient that image is. Mainstream America and its institutions aren't the problem. They're not homophobic or heterosexist. We're not like hate-filled, anti-gay crusader Fred Phelps and his family. We don't hate gay people.

Okay. Then why is it so hard to institutionalize equality in this country?

All three images somehow tried to take the sting out of what happened in Laramie, Wyoming, and of what happens regularly in this good-ole U.S.A. They also took the reality out of it all.

The play didn't take the sting out for me though. There Zubaida Ula, a passionate, inquisitive Muslim woman from Laramie, confronts us with another portrait of the events, which we, like her town, may not be willing to let sink in to replace media images. As people around her tried to claim that what happened is really out of character for their hometown, that they themselves are really not prejudiced, she objected.

"But it IS that kind of town. If it wasn't this kind of town, why did this happen here? I mean, you know what I mean, like — that's a lie. Because it happened here. So how could it not be a town where this kind of thing happens? Like that's just totally — like, looking at an Escher painting and getting all confused like, it's just totally like circular logic, like how can you even say that? And we have to mourn this and we have to be sad that we live in a town, a state, a country where shit like this happens. I mean, these are people trying to distance themselves from this crime. And we need to own this crime. I feel. Everyone needs to own it. We are like this. We ARE like this. WE are LIKE this."

She's right. No matter how we'd all like to deny it, no matter how far we'd like to distance our wholesome selves from it, we really are like this.

It Was the Summer of '03

The summer of '03 is about to become history. It's seen a whirlwind of pronouncements effecting LGBT people.

When on June 26th the Supreme Court struck down laws banning private gay sex, the justices removed a major legal obstacle cited by anti-gay extremists to deny LGBT people equal rights. The celebration was overdue but short-lived.

The angry losers in the high court's judgment ratcheted up the rhetoric, defining the next battles in their "culture wars." But they'd been doing that already this summer.

On May 15, Republican Representative Marilyn Musgrave of Colorado sponsored a Federal Marriage Amendment defining marriage for all federal, state and local government entities as "only of the union of a man and a woman." After the Court's decision, right-wing politicians climbed all over themselves this summer to sign on.

On June 17, the Southern Baptist Convention had announced that its new initiative would be to convince gay people to reject their "sinful, destructive lifestyle" and become heterosexuals just like them. Saying their public face message should be "love the sinner but hate the sin," America's largest protestant denomination, founded in 1845 to maintain slavery, continued to believe it had the moral authority to preach morality to the rest of us.

It took the SBC 150 years from its founding — safely after doing so could have made a difference during the civil rights era in the south — to finally come to the conclusion that slavery is wrong. At their 1995 Atlanta meeting, they appeared to apologize, pledging to devote the first ten years of the new millennium to eradicating racism and ethnic conflict. Only 7 more years left and then they're finished, I suppose.

On July 2, conservative retailer Walmart joined more than 300 of the top 500 U.S. companies by adding sexual orientation to its anti-discrimination policy for its 1.1 million employees.

But the "President" chose to agree with the SBC's anti-gay stance during a post-Supreme Court-decision press conference on July 30. Saying marriage was only for heterosexuals, he assured us that White House lawyers were already working on laws guaranteeing marriage's heterosexuality. He then followed with the apparently humble "we're all sinners." No matter how badly he may be a sinner (We'll grant him that.), everyone knew he too was preaching that gay people are sinners because of whom they love.

The next day, Barney Frank accused Bush of using the gay marriage issue to divert attention from Bush's failures regarding Iraq, North Korea, Liberia, the deficit, unemployment, and congressional deadlock on prescription drugs. "With President Bush's popularity dropping and the serious problems confronting America worsening, the Administration seeks to divert attention by demagoguing on the issue of same-sex unions," the Massachusetts Congressman said.

Simultaneously on July 31, the Republican Policy Committee released a policy paper prepared by Senator Jon Kyl of Arizona entitled "The Threat to Marriage from the Courts." It presents the official Republican strategy for preventing marriage equality, warning that nothing "will stop determined activists and their judicial allies [but] a constitutional amendment."

Meanwhile, July polls reflected the barrage of negative conservative attention the issue was getting following the Supreme Court decision. A CNN/USA Today poll reported that 48 percent of the respondents agreed that homosexual acts should be legal and 46 percent did not. The news headline was that public approval of homosexual activity was down from a May poll (60% approved, 35% disapproved.)

Two separate July Gallup polls detected this shift against gay rights in those who tended to be conservatives, moderates, and people who attend church. Such blips in polling aren't unusual when an issue attracts attention, and probably less significant in the long run. The long-range picture is better reflected in the fact that these polls also showed that people under age 50 are significantly more accepting of gays than their elders.

Up north, on June 18 Canadian Prime Minister Jean Chretian, after provincial courts rejected discrimination against same-sex unions, announced his party would draft a law legalizing same-sex marriage. Canadian right-wingers, as we'd expect, vowed to fight.

On the religious front, on July 4, a leading Thai Buddhist monk, Phra Payom Kalayano, called for more rigorous testing of monastic candidates to screen out homosexual men. Thai leaders, official spokesmen said, are looking into Buddhist laws to eliminate monks with "sexual deviation," declaring that they "cause trouble in the temples."

On July 31, the Vatican's Congregation for the Doctrine of the Faith, took time off from dealing with the Church's own on-going, multi-million-dollar-settlements, sexual abuse mess to release a twelve-page edict condemning "homosexual unions" and anyone who supports them. There was nothing new in the statement. "Legal recognition of homosexual unions would obscure certain basic moral values and cause a devaluation of the institution of marriage….To vote in favor of a law so harmful to the common good is gravely immoral," the document pontificated.

A week later, the President of Dignity/USA, a national organization of people who are gay and still Catholic, labeled the Vatican's actions "spiritual terrorism," an action by "the elite old-boys-club."

Not to be outdone, on August 7, right-wing televangelist Jerry Falwell announced that he was drawing a "line in the sand." He vowed to put aside everything else to devote time to passage of the constitutional ban on gay marriage.

Still, on August 4, the House of Bishops of the Episcopal Church, following a vote of approval at its General Convention in Minneapolis, voted to consecrate its first openly gay bishop Gene Robinson. It did so in spite of a last minute smear campaign by conservatives that fizzled upon investigation of the phony allegations, and amidst threats of fracturing the 77-million member worldwide Anglican Communion. Given the anger and obsession of right-wing anti-gay people with this issue, it's hard to doubt that divisions will occur.

Not to be outdone by other news, the anti-gay American Family Association acknowledged in August that Michael Johnston, the chair of "National Coming Out of Homosexuality Day" and founder of Kerusso Ministries, had undergone a "moral fall." In the tradition of a slew of ex-gay leaders Johnston, who had appeared in a national advertising campaign with his mother saying he'd "walked away from homosexuality through the power of Jesus Christ," is accused of having unprotected sex with men while failing to disclose his HIV-positive status.

So, it's already been quite a summer, hasn't it? And you can bet that there's still more to come.

What we see again, is that the movement for full acceptance and affirmation of LGBT people will continue to be successful as long as it sets the agenda. It can't merely find itself responding to the right wing. There must be a clear gay agenda.

And it will be successful if those of us who think all is well, the fight is over, and we just need to get along, pay careful attention to what's been happening. Denial didn't get LGBT people this far.

The events of the summer of '03 tell us we've come a long way. But, they also tell us we can't settle down now. Though we're getting closer, there's still a long way to go.

It's About Love: Nothing More and Nothing Less

We get distracted. The political and religious right tries its best to sidetrack us so that we're living in terms of their agenda, not ours. And they've got national think tanks to tell them how to take charge of the discussions.

Yet, there's really only one issue to discuss. Put simply in the sound bite manner that we need to repeat again and again to our culture and its media: it's the right to love whomever anyone wants to love. Period.

Why is that so hard for people to get? Maybe the real question is: Why is it so hard for us to stay on task and keep something as important as love in the forefront? Why is it so easy to get caught up in discussions that sap our energy instead of just saying that this is about the freedom to love?

It's not about whether it's a choice. In fact, why do we care whether we can or can't help being LGBT or not? The issue is irrelevant to love. Come to think of it, love is best when it is a free choice.

It's not about idealizing and achieving straight-acting relationships. Straight-acting relationships are failing all around us and disappointing heterosexual couples right and left.

It's not about whether religion and tradition affirm or reject anything at all. Down through history, we find religions and traditional ideas affirming or rejecting everything that's ever happened or been believed. And we know that often religions that have preached love have also — sometimes actually while claiming to be loving — supported deaths and war.

It's not about waiting to respond to the next right-wing initiative. It's about having a real gay agenda that's a long list of everything we want, and about relentlessly pushing the agenda.

It's not about changing the prejudices of the extreme right wing. It's about being out and about in the potentially supportive middle.

It's not about whether or not other people like us or think we're too pushy. It's about securing our equal rights and full equality.

It's not about being understood. We are complete human beings who deserve to be treated as fully human human beings whether people understand us or not.

It's not about the need to give those who don't "understand" us more time. How many generations more are we willing to give up? How many more millennia are we willing to lose to people with prejudices?

It's not about making sure that anti-gay positions are represented, as if we owe them some sort of equal opportunity. They already have the leadership of a political party, a grass roots network of thousands of churches, newspapers, magazines, radio programs, radio stations, and cable networks to get their ideas across. We've got to get over our liberal guilt about this as if we owe our abusers more "equal time."

It's not about smiling understandably while we listen to "friendly" politicians apologize to us because they can't support our issues anytime their own reelection is on the line.

It's not about being able to be quietly invisible as we work in our workplaces, learn in our educational institutions, or walk down our streets. It's about never having to hide our love by putting photos of them in our desk drawers, changing or avoiding pronouns in conversations, or remaining at a safe distance from the ones we love when we're out together.

It's not about whether or not some historical, political, or entertainment figure is LGBT. It's about our own value, and our own lives here and now.

It's not about whether our LGBT communities have dysfunctional, or down right crazy people in them. Of course, we've got messed up individuals just like every group. We have no need to apologize for them either.

It's not about our being attracted to the same sex. It's about our parents', children's, politicians', religious leaders', and institutions' homophobia, anti-LGBT prejudices, and poorly defined self-concepts.

It's not really about sex. It's about love. One of the many ways to express love is through sex, but people are not gay-bashed only while they are having sex. They are gay-bashed for showing any signs of love to the same gender.

It's not about whether or not we really like sex or we act sexually. It's not about whether we have lots of sex or none. It's not about the kinds of things we do in bed. The envy, fascination, obsession, falsifications, condemnation, and emotions expressed around LGBT sex in our society reflect our culture's own sickness about sex and pleasure. Our critics may not get this, but it's to our peril if defending ourselves centers around an issue so thoroughly confused by our culture.

It's not about whether or not the oppression of LGBT people is better or worse than racism or other oppressions. It just doesn't matter whose oppression is worse. How tacky is that argument anyway? All oppression is connected, and it's all reprehensible.

And, it's not about whether people think that talking about love is some pie-in-the-sky, far-fetched, wouldn't-it-be-nice, woo-woo, idea that our dominant war-based society considers unrealistic. If people think so, that's an expression of their own cynicism, fatalism, hopelessness, feelings of emptiness, past disappointments, failures to experience love, and inadequate upbringings.

What LGBT people are asking for is nothing more — and certainly nothing less — than changing a fear-based society to a love-based one. Few believe this can be done. Fear is so integral to our way of doing things that adults can hardly conceive of a world without it.

What we are asking for is something everyone needs, and deeply wants. Even if we don't get there soon, though, the core issue that's simple enough to be expressed over and over in sound bites, and radical enough to cause trouble, is the right for everyone to love whomever they choose.